## Praise for PARENTING

"This book is a valuable resource that clearly comes from years of practice and experience. It contains information and tools that are practical and accessible that speak to me as both a parent and a clinician."
    *Stephanie Pace, licensed clinical social worker and school counselor*

"This book is for anyone who has kids or works with kids. Sherry Walker brings massive experience and academic rigor as a clinician and teacher. But just as importantly she has an almost magic ability to fully understand a child's world. She mixes all that in a special alchemy that translates into incredibly practical and simple suggestions that everyone can implement. She shows the rubber meeting the road for improved quality of family life through easy to understand ideas and practices."
    *Julie Visnich, LCSW/LAC*

"Sherry Walker's PARENTING: WHAT WORKS WHAT WON'T AND WHY is informative, comprehensive, accessible and applicable. The anecdotes and examples Sherry shares from her many years working with children and families as a licensed therapist transform abstract principles into transformative ah-hah moments. Today's busy, often over-committed and overwhelmed parents will benefit enormously from Sherry's practical and balanced approach. This is a must-read for parents, grandparents, teachers and all those who work with children."
    *Sara Lynn Valentine, award-winning freelance writer and author of children's books, writing coach, and mom of four*

# PARENTING
## WHAT WORKS
## WHAT WON'T
## AND WHY

by Sherry F. Walker
M.C.A.T., LMFT

Surrogate Press®

Copyright ©2018 Sherry Walker

All rights reserved.

No part of this publication may be reproduced, stored in a retrieval system, or transmitted in any form or by any means, electronic, mechanical, photocopying, recording, or otherwise, without written permission of the author.

Published in the United States by
Surrogate Press®
an imprint of Faceted Press®
Surrogate Press, LLC

SurrogatePress.com

ISBN: 978-1-947459-13-7

Library of Congress Control Number: 2018935587

Book cover design by: Clint McKnight

Interior design by: Katie Mullaly, Surrogate Press®

# Table of Contents

Introduction ........................................................................................ 1

Chapter 1: General Topics on Children and Parents ...................... 7
    Myths Versus Realities About Child Rearing............................... 7
    Setting and Enforcing Behavioral Limits................................... 13
    Special Time ................................................................................. 22
    Child's Play Is Child's Work........................................................ 24
    A Child's Artwork – Significant Stages of Development
    and Appropriate Parental Response........................................... 27
    Sharing Literature With the Child – Story Books, Fables,
    Myths, and Old-Fashioned Fairy Tales..................................... 31
    Productive Problem-Solving Discussions
    and Role Modeling for Parents .................................................. 35
    Top Tips to Help Parents and Children
    Get Along With Each Other....................................................... 38
    Preparing for the Arrival of a New Baby ................................... 41

Chapter 2: Overview of Child Development ................................. 44
    Non-Verbal Language ................................................................. 44
    Piaget and Cognitive Development........................................... 46
    Freud, Erikson, and Psychoanalytic Theory.............................. 47
    Thinking, Sensing and Feelings, Making Action Decisions,
    and *The Wizard of Oz* as a Metaphor ....................................... 52

Chapter 3: The First Eighteen Months of Life ............................... 56
    Pregnancy, Birth, and First Month of the Infant's Life ........... 56
    Thinking and Paying Attention.................................................. 58
    Language and Music Development ........................................... 61
    Sensing and Feelings: Assessing Responsibility........................ 63

    Making Decisions and Taking Action ........................................................... 65

    Activities ........................................................................................................... 69

    Family Life ........................................................................................................ 71

    Self-Image – If All Goes Well Enough ......................................................... 71

    Difficulties Linked to This Stage That May Emerge Later ...................... 72

Chapter 4: Eighteen to Thirty-Six Months of Life .......................................... 73

    Use of Energy .................................................................................................. 73

    Thinking and Paying Attention .................................................................... 73

    Verbal Language Development .................................................................... 75

    Physical Development ................................................................................... 78

    Sensing and Feelings: Assessing Responsibility ........................................ 78

    Making Decisions and Taking Action ........................................................ 80

    Family Life ....................................................................................................... 84

    Activities ........................................................................................................... 85

    Self-Image – If All Goes Well Enough ......................................................... 87

    Difficulties Linked to This Stage That May Emerge Later ...................... 88

Chapter 5: Three to Six Years of Age ................................................................. 90

    Use of Energy .................................................................................................. 90

    Thinking, Paying Attention, and Learning ................................................ 90

    Language Development and Music Development .................................. 94

    Sensing and Feelings: Assessing Responsibility ........................................ 96

    Physical Development ................................................................................... 99

    Making Decisions and Taking Actions .................................................... 100

    Family Life ..................................................................................................... 101

    Activities ......................................................................................................... 103

    Self-Image – If All Goes Well Enough ....................................................... 112

    Difficulties Linked to This Stage That May Emerge Later .................... 113

Chapter 6: Latency: Six Years of Age to Puberty ........................................... 114

    Use of Energy ................................................................................................ 114

    Thinking, Paying Attention, and Learning .............................................. 114

    Sensing and Feelings: Assessing Responsibility ............ 117

    Making Decisions and Taking Action ............ 119

    School ............ 120

    Family Life ............ 122

    Changes That Occur Two Years Before Puberty ............ 126

    Situations That Should Be Addressed
If They Occur During this Stage ............ 127

    Self-Perception – If Things Go Well Enough ............ 137

    Difficulties Linked to This Stage
That May Emerge or Worsen Now and/or Later ............ 138

    Activities ............ 139

Chapter 7: Adolescence ............ 140

    Overall View of Adolescence ............ 140

    The Stages of Adolescence ............ 141

    Use of Physical Energy ............ 143

    Reworking of the Hallmark Skills of the
First Stage of Development ............ 143

    Reworking of the Hallmark Skills of the
Second Stage of Development ............ 146

    Reworking of the Hallmark Skills of the
Third Stage of Development ............ 149

    The Ending of Adolescence ............ 155

    Self-Perception – If Things Go Well Enough ............ 155

    Difficulties Originating in This or Earlier Stages
That May Appear in Adolescence or Later ............ 156

In Closing ............ 160

Acknowledgments ............ 162

About the Author ............ 163

# Introduction

There are no scholarly citations in this writing. It's a compilation of information about children, parents, and child rearing gathered from many sources over the past sixty years that I, and some others, have found useful. I hope that some of the information will be of help to those of you on the challenging but rewarding journey of raising children. It is a winding path with moments of intense joy, periods of quiet satisfaction, and moments when you may be brought to your knees in despair and confusion.

My hope in writing this is to increase awareness of the differences between the ways that children and adults think and experience the world, in order to improve effective communication between them. That is to say, I hope to increase the chance that what each attempts to convey to the other is close to the message received.

Parents readily accept the entire responsibility of learning to correctly interpret the meaning of their infant's sounds and actions. They (the parents) have more difficulty recognizing that they must continue to shoulder the majority of this responsibility until the child:

1. Is able to recognize what is real and what isn't (between four and six years of age).
2. Can communicate well with verbal language and understands that words can convey more than just their literal meaning (at about five years of age).
3. Is able to think abstractly (between nine and eleven years of age).

Until the child possesses these abilities, parents and their children inhabit two very different perceptual worlds.

Nonverbal behavior is the universal first language of human beings. Infants and young children lack the ability to perceive and think about events in words. Their language, therefore, is movement. This nonverbal *language* powerfully shapes the early critical years when the child's perceptions of *who* he or she *is* as an individual—and what he or she might expect of him/herself and of the world—are forming. Children learn, almost from birth, that certain events, objects, and behaviors are connected. This may occur long before they understand the true nature of such connections. The extent to which the child is influenced by early nonverbal learning fades from conscious awareness as the ability to think in, and use, words takes over. That early nonverbal learning remains, nevertheless, deeply ingrained, as fully integrated to a child's sense of self and as difficult to change as the barb deeply embedded in the center of a fully-grown tree, a tree which, in its earliest years, had no choice but to grow around a section of a barbed wire fence.

Behavior (*action speaking louder than words*) continues to provide powerful emotional context in human communication throughout life. Every action has two aspects that occur simultaneously. The *functional* aspect refers to *what* action is being taken. The *qualitative* aspect refers to *how* that action is performed. For example, two people place a forkful of meat into their respective mouths. One person stabs his fork into the meat and quickly jams the food into his mouth. The other person plays lightly with the meat with her fork before leisurely and gently placing it in her mouth. *What* each did was functionally the same, but *how* it was done was qualitatively different—therefore, very divergent *meanings* may be attached to these functionally similar actions.

What this means on a practical level is that whenever there's a disparity between what someone says and his or her accompanying nonverbal behavior, we receive and we believe the nonverbal message. Suppose your employer verbally assures you that she really wants to hear your ideas about improving the company's business practices. If she is sitting behind her desk with arms and legs crossed and brows knit, you would wisely doubt the sincerity of her words, and proceed to offer suggestions with caution.

Parents need to be aware that actions do indeed speak louder than words—and parents must try to avoid, in the communication they model with each other and with their children, disparity between spoken communication and accompanying nonverbal behavior. An apology offered with a scowl by someone who doesn't feel at all sorry for his behavior is not credible. Nor is the statement from an adult who has just made a sarcastic remark about her partner's behavior, when she adds, as a smirking disclaimer of negative intent, "I was just kidding."

Recognition of how differently adults and young children perceive any given situation can reduce confusion for parents, help them avoid conflict, and make the parent/child relationship more enjoyable. Following are several examples of how the differences in a parent's perception and a child's perception—the sometimes vast gulf between their separate *realities*—can lead to miscommunication.

I was standing next to a three-year-old in a delicatessen while her mother was ordering lunch at the counter. The child couldn't take her eyes off the ten-foot-long, fake swordfish mounted on the wall behind the counter. She became increasingly upset. I leaned over and told her that the swordfish couldn't be real, because if it was, the whole store would be filled up with water, because real fish only live in water. The child heaved a great sigh of relief.

A four-year-old living in a high rise apartment in Chicago, who passionately wants a pony for her birthday, may assure a parent that she is going to get one. Her absolute belief is based on the intensity of her desire to receive a pony, and this overrides all parental explanations about why this cannot happen. The child's absolute belief makes no sense to her parents, whose thinking is based on reality, not on the intensity of wishes.

In another *separate reality* scenario, when feeling angry, just like Max in Maurice Sendak's book, *Where The Wild Things Are*, the child may believe that he actually IS that Wild Thing. (After Max is banished to his bedroom for bad behavior, he is transported to a world where he is celebrated as a Wild Thing. However, he soon starts to feel lonely and decides to return home, where a hot supper awaits him.) The child may also perceive that his mother, when angry, turns into a monster resembling the mean and nasty beasts in Sendak's book. Look closely at the illustrations—do you recognize which wild things are Max's parents? A young child will gladly point them out to you.

Halloween costumes often terrify children, because they signal a total and troubling transformation of the familiar person the child watched put on the costume. Similarly, from a young child's perspective, a broken cookie couldn't possibly taste the same as one that is intact. The single, observable, physical difference between the intact and the broken cookie convinces the child that the two cookies must have other *divergent* qualities as well, such as different tastes.

Remembering some misperceptions you yourself had as a young child will help you better understand. For example, my parents had an elderly friend who drank a cup of hot tea each morning, which she referred to as her *eye opener*. This lady had one drooping eyelid, and I remember following her about in the mornings when I was a young child, hoping to see her pour the tea onto her eye to treat the droopy eyelid!

Fortunately, by five or six years of age a child's ability to understand and use verbal language has vastly improved. Once a child is communicating verbally, asking the child directly why he or she thinks an event has occurred, or what the child thinks might happen next, provides valuable insight into the child's perceptual world and what meanings the child has attached to events.

For example, four-year-old Billy's parents were alarmed when their mild-mannered son repeatedly tried to kick his eight-month-pregnant mother in the belly. The parents, increasingly desperate, tried various suggestions from other parents, teachers, and the school counselor. Nothing worked. Finally, one night after Billy had been sharply reprimanded for trying to deliver a healthy kick to his mother's pregnant belly, Billy burst into tears and cried out, "But you like it when the baby kicks!"

Seven-year-old Shelley provides another example of the need to ask a child what meaning he or she has attributed to words spoken by parents or significant others. When Shelly asked her parents where babies came from her parents quickly consulted books on the subject and solicited tips from other parents, then gave their daughter *the most comfortable explanation they could put together.* They were quite surprised when, after all of their efforts, Shelley asked, "But where do babies *really* come from? Brian's little baby sister came from Chicago."

Indeed, Brian's parents had recently flown to that city to pick up the infant girl they were adopting. Shelley's parents could have responded more quickly to Shelley's question by asking her where she thought babies came from, or even why she was thinking about where babies came from.

Here are two examples of the world as perceived by the young child *who is verbal*, but who can comprehend only the literal meaning of words.

Two-year-old Matthew was attempting to build a tower in the middle of the room with four-inch square foam blocks. The tower fell down every time a fourth block was added. Observing his son's increasing frustration, Matthew's father said, "You can make a higher tower if you put the blocks against the wall as you build."

Matthew gave his father a look of delighted discovery, grabbed two blocks and held them against the wall about two feet off the ground. When he let go of the blocks, they fell straight to the floor. Matthew shot his father a withering look, a clear statement of his disappointment in his father's poor judgment. Matthew had taken his father's words literally. The abstract idea of bracing a structure by giving it additional support was beyond Matthew.

Two-year-old blond, curly haired Lisa and her mother were in a hardware store. A lady advanced towards them, leaned down towards Lisa, and in a loud voice asked, "What's your name?" Lisa was startled, and didn't respond.

"My, what a pretty little tow-head!" exclaimed the lady (referring to Lisa's blond hair). Lisa's eyes were wide as she raised her hands and felt around her head, to ascertain whether there was a toe on her head.

"What's the matter, cat got your tongue?" boomed the lady. Lisa's hands flew to her mouth to see if a cat had indeed taken her tongue. Lisa's mother reassured her daughter that she didn't have a toe on her head, that a cat hadn't gotten her tongue, and that the aggressive lady had a problem of not knowing how to appropriately talk with little children. Lisa was too young to know that although some words sound exactly like other words, they may have different meanings (tow and toe). She didn't know that idiomatic *sayings* (cat got your tongue) may have meanings very different from their literal definitions.

The ability to think abstractly doesn't develop until somewhere between nine and eleven years of age. Abstract thinking allows the individual to take into consideration things that lie beyond physical reality, such as emotions, theories, rules, and values.

Until this ability develops, the child's thinking does not extend beyond physical existence. Wise parents take this into consideration—not doing so can be a major impediment to good communication between parent and child.

For example, telling twenty-five-month-old Max to "Be nice to your guest" won't prevent Max from hitting his guest when the guest won't relinquish the toy with which Max wants to play. Max cannot yet understand that the other child has feelings and will naturally be upset when Max hits him. Because Max cannot see, hear, taste, or touch the other child's feelings, they don't exist for Max, therefore Max is not yet capable of feeling true remorse for hitting his guest. The only effective way at this point for his parents to deal with Max's unacceptable behavior is for them to make it clear they won't allow Max to hit the other child—and to physically separate Max from the toy and/or other child for a short time.

Six-year-old Sue consistently cheated when playing board games, even after assuring her parents that this time she was going to *play fair*. Despite her parents' concerns, Sue was not destined for a life of crime! She simply hadn't yet gained the ability to understand abstract concepts such as fairness, honesty, and mutual trust. Her behavior greatly annoyed her older siblings. Only if Sue agreed to abide by the rules of the game was she was allowed to enter into a game with her siblings—and at the first sign of cheating, she was removed from the game. When playing with just her parents, however, Sue got to choose if cheating was to be allowed, and if so, whether everyone, or just Sue, was allowed to cheat.

Although too young for abstract thinking, the child does perceive that she is part of the physical world around her, and she therefore believes that she has some part in causing all that occurs in her environment. For example, when a child's parents are arguing with each other in angry voices, the child assumes that he or she was, at least to some extent, the cause of the parents' anger. In reality the parents' anger may have little or nothing to do with the child.

Seven-year-old Mark's parents repeatedly tried to reassure him that their upcoming divorce had nothing to do with him. Mark learned to tell people that he knew that the divorce was not his fault, as his parents kept telling him—but in reality, he did believe that he was at fault. Mark couldn't do otherwise than reason that in some unknown way he was responsible, at least in part, given that he and his parents had all been living together in the same physical location.

Until Mark acquired the ability to think abstractly, his parents could only try to reassure him only by regularly reminding him that even though children often believe they caused their parents' divorce, wise adults know that only adults can cause divorces.

# General Topics on Children and Parents
## Chapter 1

### Myths Versus Realities About Child Rearing

1. Myth: Parents will always have loving feelings for their child.

    Reality: There will be many times when parents are so upset with their child's behavior that they may even reach the point of wondering if they will ever again feel lovingly towards their child.

2. Myth: If parents want to raise a caring child, they should bend over backwards to always be nice to the child, even in circumstances when the child is not treating the parents well.

    Reality: The child learns by example. It is important for the child to see his or her parents insist on good treatment from the important people in their lives, including the child. That models for the child that he or she also should expect and insist upon good treatment from others.

3. Myth: The way to encourage a child to tell parents about emotionally important events in the child's life is for the parents to take every opportunity to ask the child about emotionally important events in the child's life.

    Reality: A balance needs to be struck between how much interest each shows in the life of the other. Asking about events or offering to share about events are important, but it is also important for both parent and child to have the option to not share. At times parent, child, or both may desire some time to privately reflect on events before being asked to share them.

    If you wish to hear more about your child's life, try sharing one positive and one negative emotionally charged event in your day for about two weeks, without inquiring about the child's life at all. After that, tell your child that you would love to hear about the best—and the yuckiest—thing that happened in his or her day. Remember, that which is emotionally charged, not just the bare facts of the day's events, is most interesting to a child. The child is often interested in *yucky* things that occurred in the parents' own childhoods, as well as in their current lives. A child is far less interested in hearing about positive events.

4. Myth: You will love and understand all of your children equally, and in the same way.

   Reality: The genetic predispositions that influence the unique ways different individuals attribute meaning to experiences, along with naturally occurring differences in personality, make it unlikely that you will respond to and care about each child in exactly the same way. Think of adults with whom you have regular contact; you naturally gravitate towards some and not towards others. The understanding and love you experience for each of your children will probably ebb and flow throughout the childrearing years.

5. Myth: It is wise to keep all marital and family difficulties from the child and assure the child all is fine.

   Reality: Children are extremely sensitive to the emotional atmosphere in the home. It is not helpful for the child to be told that nothing is wrong when the child, fluent in the language of nonverbal behavior, knows this is not true. However, how much parents tell a child about current difficulties should depend on the child's developmental age.

   For example, a seven-year-old can be told, "Right now Mommy and Daddy are not having a good time together, but we are trying to get things better between us. We are grownups and believe that nothing you did or did not do caused this problem. We believe that only grownups can cause these problems, and only grownups have the responsibility to try to fix them."

   A fourteen-year-old can be told, "I've been worried about our financial situation, and I am working on a plan to help. That's made me cranky with you. I just want you to know that you haven't done anything to cause my bad mood, and I'm sorry that it's been landing on you."

   If there are significant and ongoing difficulties in family life, parents should seek professional help from a licensed psychotherapist. Even if the parents believe that the child's behavior is, in fact, the main source of difficulty, it is best if they make it clear that they are seeking help because *they*, the parents, want to change how things are going in the family. It is never helpful to say to the child, "Your behavior is unacceptable, and we're taking you to see a therapist to get you straightened out."

6. Myth: Parents must always agree with one another when setting up rules and limits for the child.

    Reality: The child is almost always acutely aware of differences in opinion between his parents. If they have different ideas, the parents need to inform the child which of the parent's rules will apply in a given situation. For example, the parents can back one another up when the child jumps on the bed on a night when Mom is in charge of bedtime because the child knows that although Dad *does* allow this when he is in charge, Mom *does not*.

    It is particularly unhelpful when one parent gives lip service support to behavioral demands of the other parent for the child while actually undermining the efforts of the other parent. For example: Mother to child: "Your room has to be cleaned up before you go out to play today."

    Undermining Father (in a tone conveying total lack of conviction): "Your mother says you have to clean up your room before you go out to play today."

7. Myth: Children should be left alone to learn to resolve their differences by themselves.

    Reality: A child's brain matures at such a rapid pace that his entire way of thinking about events changes dramatically about every two years. This is evidenced by the tremendous gains in ability to use verbal language. Letting a six- and eight-year-old, with their very different cognitive abilities try, to resolve an emotionally hot issue is unlikely to work. Better to have a family rule that children should try to use words to resolve a problem between them, but if that fails, ask for adult help. In this case, such support should be available.

    This doesn't mean that the parent becomes embroiled in every situation, trying to figure out which child was at fault. Nor does it mean that tattling is encouraged. It does mean that an adult's perspective can be sought when a bridge needs to be forged between children of different cognitive abilities.

    For example, two-year-old Jake constantly messed up everything his five-year-old brother Marcus set up with his toys. Jake was only interested in the toys which Marcus was playing. The parents reassured Marcus that in a few months Jake would be a better playmate, but that in the meantime, Marcus could announce "Jake alert!" when necessary, and the parents would remove Jake to another location and activity without recriminations to either child. This preserved positive feelings between the children. Within a few days of the implementation of this plan, Jake could be seen slumping in resignation whenever his brother announced "Jake alert!" He had quickly learned that these words meant he, Jake, would immediately be carted away!

As a general rule, the younger the children, and the greater the age difference between the children, the more likely adult intervention will be needed to resolve conflicts. The adult can help resolve a conflict by making it clear that the word *you* cannot be used by either disputant. Each child can only speak about what was seen, heard, or what happened to the child himself. When the word *you* is forbidden, no one can be attacked or blamed. Discussion and resolution of the situation become possible. With an adult present to enforce this rule, the attack, "You took my toy and I hate you!" can be changed to a statement about the speaker's situation, such as, "I hate it when my toy gets taken!"

8. Myth: Parents can count on grandparents to be enthusiastic about caring for grandchildren on a regular basis.

    Reality: It is wise to talk about what involvement would be desirable and/or acceptable to both parents and grandparents-to-be before grandchildren are born. Some grandparents have, for many years, eagerly anticipated being involved grandparents while others have eagerly looked forward to time to devote to their own adult pursuits.

9. Myth: New parents' troubled relationships with *their* own parents will improve once they have children; the elder parents will acknowledge the younger parents' status as adults.

    Reality: Whether this occurs or not has a lot to do with the relationships established prior to the arrival of the first grandchild. It will be helpful to have a direct and open discussion of the expectations each generation of parents attaches to the advent of a grandchild. This can lead to both parents-to-be and grandparents-to-be having realistic expectations for their future relationship. Difficulties are sure to arise if, for instance, grandparents believe they have the authority to override the younger parents' authority in disciplining the grandchild—or if the young parents assume grandparents will be happy to babysit whenever the parents request it.

10. Myth: Parents can expect support for their style of parenting from the grandparents.

    Reality: Parents and grandparents often have different ideas about parenting. They need to agree upon whose rules will be enforced when the three generations are together. The rules may (or may not) differ, depending on whether the child is in the parents' home versus the grandparents' home. These rules need to be made clear to the child.

    For instance, when ten-year-old Betsy is alone with Grandma at Grandma's house, Betsy may be allowed to skip eating vegetables, and stay up much later than when home with her parents. When Grandma visits Betsy's home, Betsy's parents' rules about eating and bedtime apply. Children are quite capable of accepting that different rules apply in different situations as long as they know who is in charge and which and whose rules apply.

11. Myth: Parents should be proud of their child's accomplishments.

    Reality: It is the child who has accomplished something; he or she may or may not feel proud about having done so. Ask the child how he feels about what he has done. This encourages the child to develop a sense of self-worth and agency. If you and the child disagree about his accomplishment, acknowledge that difference rather than insisting that you both feel the same way. For example, "You and I have different ideas about the haircut you gave yourself. You love the haircut but I'll miss seeing the braid you cut off. However, I'll learn to live with your haircut, even though I don't like it. And, of course, I still love you." This kind of statement focuses on what has occurred, not on the motivation or personality of the child.

12. Myth: The child will be grateful if you give him or her all the exact advantages that you were not given when you were growing up.

    Reality: Perhaps your parents never provided you with the piano lessons you craved. You therefore try to make up for this by ensuring that your child has piano lessons. However, if your child has no interest whatsoever in music lessons, it will not register as an advantage to him or her. Providing a child with opportunity to pursue his or her own interest is the real issue.

13. Myth: Parenting comes naturally to most parents and they feel skilled and confident most of the time about the way they are raising their children.

    Reality: Most parents are regularly beset with small, medium, and large questions and doubts about their parenting, and these doubts continue throughout the child-rearing years.

14. Myth: Having a child will improve an unsatisfactory relationship between the parents.

    Reality: In very rare instances this does happen, but having a child will most likely exacerbate preexisting conflicts as well as introduce new challenges.

15. Myth: It is best to appear to have complete confidence in your own judgment, so never reveal to your child that you have doubts about something you said or about a consequence you applied in response to the child's unacceptable behavior.

    Reality: Telling your child you are sorry but allowing your actions to communicate a different message is always a bad idea. However, if you later truly regret something that you said or did (for example, "You'll never ride your bike again"), and are fairly sure you will not repeat it, acknowledging your regret can be quite helpful. It takes some pressure off the child to know that even an adult can admit making mistakes and take corrective action. But be aware: when you, the parent, admit you have made a mistake and intend to change your behavior, your child will be watching to see if you follow through.

16. Myth: When the child misbehaves, the parent should try to get the child to explain why he or she did what was done and how he or she feels about it.

    Reality: Children are rarely able, when pressured by a displeased parent, to articulate exactly why they took a certain action or how they feel about it. It is more helpful to apply consequences, if necessary, and leave any discussion about the child's thoughts and feelings for a later, less emotionally charged moment.

17. Myth: Parents should always put the child's needs first; to do otherwise is to be selfish.

Reality: There is a huge difference between being selfish and being self-caring. Many of us were raised with the message that putting ourselves first is never acceptable, that such behavior is selfish. Remember that to the child it looks like a lot of work is ahead for him before he reaches adulthood. So it is encouraging to the child to see that on occasion, in the absence of the child's immediate need (e.g. illness), it can be appropriate for adults to put their needs and desires first.

It is important to set and observe suitable boundaries for occasions when the parent attends to his or her own interests, as opposed to occasions when the focus is on the child's needs and interests. For example, eleven-year-old Jack's parents wanted to make sure he never felt left out or unimportant, so they consistently allowed him to interrupt their telephone calls and join in on their adult conversations with each other.

When limits were eventually set on Jack's participation in adult conversations, he said he felt relieved that his parents didn't seem to need him so much anymore. When his parents complimented him on his newly acquired patience and self-sufficiency during times when they were attending to matters between themselves, Jack's confidence and self-esteem soared.

## Setting and Enforcing Behavioral Limits

Having several consistently enforced, general family rules can be helpful. This works best when the rules are applied to the behavior of all family members. Here are three suggestions that cover a great deal of what can occur between family members:

a) No hurting of bodies.

b) No put downs, i.e., no hurting of feelings.

c) No taking anyone else's belongings without prior permission of the owner. This is easier to enforce if each person involved has at least a shelf or a box in which to store things he or she does not wish to share.

Suppose one child hits another child. If the child who has been hit doesn't retaliate physically, but instead comes to the parent for help, the parent is on solid ground to support that child. However, if the child who was initially hit retaliates physically, the parent is on solid ground to level a consequence on both children for breaking a family rule. For instance, if George hits Peter, who then hits George back, a parent might say, "I'm going to put my children in separate rooms for a while because they both broke the family rule about not hurting bodies."

Unfortunately, when a child misbehaves, parental response often focuses on the child as a person, rather than on the improper behavior. For instance, "Why did you do that?" Or, "What got into you?" "How can you be so stupid?" It is less damaging to the child's self-esteem when parents focus solely on the child's immediate unacceptable behavior, attempting to find a consequence that will encourage the child to make a different behavioral choice in the future.

An even more effective way to address misbehavior is for the parent to keep the focus on him or herself. For example, Molly's mother told Molly, "I was very upset when Miss Clark told me about my daughter's behavior at school today. I am still so upset that I am going to take this afternoon to read my book. That will help me get into a better mood. So our planned trip to the mall to buy you a new shirt is cancelled."

Molly's mother hoped that her daughter's dismay about the cancelled shopping trip would equal in emotional magnitude the dismay she, Molly's mother, felt upon hearing about her daughter's misbehavior at school. She hoped the result would be that her daughter would refrain from such behavior in the future.

The consequence imposed by the parent should impact the child in some unhappy way, but *only* the child. The parent might say, "I don't have energy to read any stories to you tonight." But if reading to the child at night is in fact a great pleasure for the parent, the consequence lands on the parent as well as on the child. The parent might better strike a middle ground by saying, "Cleaning up your spilled juice this morning I used up the energy I was going to use to read you *two* stories tonight, so I'll only have energy to read *one* story tonight." Similarly, rather than saying, "Because the family member responsible for dishwashing didn't do his job, family night at the movies is cancelled," the parent might better say, "The family member who didn't do his job won't be having dessert tonight."

Unfortunately, as parents we have all lost it and lashed out at one time or another when confronted with our child's unacceptable behavior. Parents often put their child in time-out when the child is upset and boils over. Parents need to consider doing the same with themselves. A productive discussion is impossible when one or both parties are extremely upset.

It is wise to refrain from stating what action the parent is going to take in response to a child's misbehavior when the parent is still extremely upset. This helps the parent avoid locking himself into an angry response that might, in retrospect, seem too harsh for the situation. By contrast, talking about what action the parent *feels* like taking does no harm. For example, "Right now I *feel* like taking your bicycle away for the whole summer!" Or, "Right now I'm too upset to decide *what* I'm going to do about this situation, so I'm going to wait until I've calmed down to make a decision." Although very difficult to make in the heat of the moment, this type of response is well worth the effort.

*You* is one of the most upsetting words in the English language when used by someone who is displeased by the behavior of another. It is universally heard as an attack upon the person being addressed as "you," and its use is never helpful. Unfortunately, it's almost reflexive for parents to employ the *you* word. Most (if not all) of us have been accused of misdeeds both rightly and wrongly by adults who liberally sprinkled their complaints about us with the *you* word.

Some interesting things, however, happen when that word is avoided with intentionality. The parent is left talking about himself, how he feels about the unsatisfactory situation that confronts him, how he intends to ameliorate the situation and restore himself to a better emotional state. This requires so much cognitive effort that the upset parent tends to speak much more slowly and, as a result, makes more careful word choices. This increases the chance that the child will actually pay attention to (hear) what the parent is saying. An additional benefit of parents embracing this practice is that it models for the child appropriate and extraordinarily helpful behavior in the face of conflict.

It is important for parents to limit the scope of their complaints to a child's specific unacceptable behavior. When Greta leaves a single chore undone and her mother says, "Greta, I better see more responsible behavior or there's going to be big trouble," the scope of the mother's apparent dissatisfaction appears unproductively broad, not specific enough.

It is important to let the child know that the parent fully loves the person the child is, and is only upset about the child's specific behavior. A child younger than seven or eight cannot separate the way he perceives and feels about himself from the way he feels about a particular action he takes. If a six-year-old is chastised for striking out in a baseball game, the child is not upset because he struck out, he is upset because he feels that he himself, his whole being, is a *strike out*. This is why it is best to wait until children are at least seven before enrolling them in competitive sports.

Empty threats directed at a child do not lead to positive behavioral change. The child quickly learns to disregard them, relegating them to the realm of annoying adult background noise. Use of bribes, public embarrassment, sarcasm, judgmental language and insults all exacerbate negative feelings between parent and child and rarely lead to desired behavioral changes. For example, berating a child with "There you go again, being stupid and thoughtless, just like your uncle Mark" is highly unlikely to produce a positive behavioral response.

Saying what *is* and is *not* acceptable to you is more effective than going on and on about right and wrong or good and bad. For example, "Leaving dirty dishes in the sink is not acceptable to me!" versus "It is just plain *wrong and bad* to leave dirty dishes in the sink!"

Rewarding the child is not a good strategy for motivating desirable everyday behavior. Rewards should be reserved for situations in which the child puts forth unexpected or extraordinary effort or performance.

We have all heard a child say "I'm sorry" in a tone reeking with insincerity, after being ordered by an adult to apologize. If the child isn't at all remorseful about what she has done, forcing her to apologize and say "I'm sorry" just trains the child to lie. It is more helpful to insist that the child say that she will try not to repeat the unacceptable action for a reasonable length of time. This time will vary, given the age of the offender. Having the child say she will *never* repeat the unacceptable action is unrealistic, and, again, teaches the child to speak insincerely.

How the child *feels* about what he or she has done should be left to the child. However, it is up to the parent to determine whether the way in which the child expresses and communicates his feelings with *actions* is acceptable or not. For example, Harry decided to express his anger at his sister by throwing the contents of her dollhouse onto the floor. Their father helped his daughter restore the contents of the dollhouse, and decided that he would best recover from his anger at his son if he didn't have to see him for an hour or so, so he sent Harry to his room. En route to his room, Harry stomped his feet as loudly as he possibly could on every stair. His wise father chose to pay attention to Harry's *actions* (moving towards his room) and not to Harry's *attitude* (stomping loudly on every stair).

It is important to distinguish between a request and a demand. A request can be declined but a demand cannot. A young child will probably not be aware of the moral imperative implied by "Can you please clean up your toys now?" The child may answer "Yes" but make no move to clean up the toys. Remember that children do not thinks like adults, and the young child may have understood the parent to be asking if the child was physically capable of cleaning up the toys.

An older child might respond "No, I don't want to." In this case she may be responding to what she understood to be a request that can be accepted or declined. When the parents say, "I have to have the toys cleaned up right now," it is clearly a demand and not a request.

For a child older than seven or eight years of age who ignores the parent's demand to stop a particular behavior, the concept of a *worser* may help. A worser, the parent can explain, is something worse than what the child would ordinarily expect, that *may* occur if the unwanted behavior continues.

If at all possible, behavioral expectations should be made clear to a child before he is in a potentially problematic situation. The parent should always take the child's developmental stage into consideration. Telling a three-year-old to "behave himself at Aunt Sally's" lacks focus and clarity. What will and won't be allowed at Aunt Sally's must be spelled out. For example, he can play with his toys in the living room where the adults will be talking, but he will have to go to another room to play with his noisy fire engine.

If a child older than seven or eight misbehaves in a situation where it is inappropriate for the parent to immediately implement a consequence, the parent can decide to get through the current situation with as much grace as possible, saving the consequence announcement for later. Once at home, the parent can spell out the consequence. For instance, mother might say to daughter "I took my daughter to the mall to get her shoes. However, her behavior there was unacceptable to me. I'm unwilling to take the chance of experiencing that behavior again, so I will be watching the new video by myself this evening."

Did you notice how the *you* word was avoided? The child is likely to vociferously object to such a consequence, protesting that, "You didn't tell me that would happen if I acted up in the mall!" The parent can truthfully reply, "As a parent, I have the responsibility to prepare my child to hold a job when my child is grown up. If my child fails to accomplish an assigned job, her boss may be unwilling to let her try to do the job again. He may, instead, just fire her. Therefore, I must prepare her to face consequences that can't be known in advance."

There can be no meaningful contract between any two people, in any situation, unless both have a clear understanding and agreement about who is going to do what and when. If you have a partner, do you have a contract about what constitutes cleaning up after dinner or getting the children ready for school? A lot of family clashes can be avoided by negotiating clear contracts detailing how daily situations should be handled. A business would fail if the owner simply asked a supplier to send him the widgets he needs as soon as possible. A written agreement takes the guesswork out of how many widgets the supplier will send and when they will arrive, leading to an efficient and predictable outcome.

Telling a child to clean his room without the kind of basic details that might be specified in a contract is usually too vague. Be sure the child knows how the parent expects the room to look once the task is done. The parent might hang a picture or diagram of how the room should look when the task is completed, make a list of the steps that must be taken, or break the job down into parts and have the child check in for approval as each part is completed.

Setting an audibly clicking kitchen timer and challenging the child to try to beat the clock (by accomplishing part of the task before the bell rings) can also be helpful. The parent might choose to work alongside a child under five years of age—as he or she puts the toy cars away the parent might gather up the building blocks while providing companionship. Doing so changes the focus from a large, daunting, and perhaps intimidating project to an opportunity for the child to experience the pleasure of teamwork and the satisfaction and self-esteem gained from a job well done. Little self-esteem, however, will result from an assigned job that is only accomplished through continual parental reminders.

For a child nine or more years old, a time frame should be established for when the task is to be completed. The parent should say nothing until that time limit has been reached. If only part of an assigned task has been done correctly or completely, the parent can comment positively on that part first, then move on to discussing what remains to be done, or, if necessary, to what consequences will come into play. For example, "I'm happy to see that the toys have been put away, but clothes must also be put away before there is any computer time."

At times, children appear to purposefully try to provoke parents beyond their endurance. Although annoying and upsetting to parents, there is often a good reason for the child's behavior. Children are frequently pushed beyond their own emotional endurance, when, for example, they are forbidden to interrupt their parents' seemingly endless conversations, told to have a good attitude about leaving the playground before their friends have to, or commanded to *understand* that baby sisters don't mean any harm when they continually knock down carefully constructed block structures. By pushing parents beyond their own endurance, the child is asking the parent to model effective steps that the child might himself need to take.

When children make behavioral choices that are unsatisfactory to parents, it's the parents' responsibility to inform them how and why their behavior was unsatisfactory and to suggest alternative, more acceptable behavior. It is a good idea for the parent, before reacting to unsatisfactory behavior, to ask why the child thought the behavior was appropriate.

For example, four-year-old Erick had been busy at the easel applying green paint to a large piece of paper. He had decided to also paint his arms and hands green. His mother told him to wash the paint off his arms and hands and then to join his brother to help mix cookie dough with their hands. His mother was distracted for a few minutes by a telephone call. When she returned and looked into the bowl of cookie dough, she saw that two of the four hands mixing it were green—that, in fact, some of the cookie dough had turned an unfortunate shade of green. She was not happy. She asked Erick if he remembered what she had just told him. He responded, "Sure, wash my arms and hands, and then mix the cookie dough with my hands. As soon as I finish mixing the cookie dough, I'll wash." The order in which things are to be done can be reversed without consequence in the mind of a four-year-old. Erick believed that he was following his mother's directions.

Parental response to the child's unacceptable behavior should be tailored to the personality of the child. One child responds well simply to a tone of disapproval in the parent's voice. Another child may need to experience the loss of an anticipated pleasure. For example, twelve-year-old Harriet and her mother agreed that Harriet would clean up her room by two o'clock in the afternoon, after which her mother would drive Harriet to visit her best friend. When the room wasn't cleaned up by two o'clock, Harriet's mother told her, "I am going to take a long walk to recover from my upset that my daughter didn't honor the agreement I had with her, so I won't be able to drive her to her friend's house until I return from my walk."

Parents, don't ask the question if you already know the answer. If you know that Amelia ate the cookies, don't ask, "Who ate all of the cookies?" If you don't know whether or not Amelia ate the cookies and you want her to tell the truth, you have to make it more worthwhile for her to tell you the truth than to lie about what she did. For example: "I want to know if my daughter Amelia ate all of the cookies. If she ate them and I hear the truth from my daughter about this, the consequence will be less harsh than if she lies about this."

Parental response to lying also must to be tailored to the child's developmental stage. If the parent is fairly sure that his six-year-old is lying when she says, "Mommy said I could eat all of the cookies before lunch," trouble may be avoided by the parent asking, "Is that what Mommy will say when I ask her about this?"

A dad might well respond to an older child's lie by saying, "I find it difficult to believe that your mother gave you permission to stay at the mall until ten p.m. Are you sure you want me to call her right now and ask her about it?"

It works out best if the parent keeps his focus on clarifying what is unacceptable about the immediate situation and why and how he is taking steps both to improve the situation and to alleviate his own upset about what has occurred. For example: "This is the third argument I have heard my children having in the last half hour, so I'm going to put my children in separate rooms for a while so that I won't be hearing any more arguments for a while."

Think of your own response to someone expressing intense anger towards your behavior. It is likely that you would immediately want to: distance yourself from the situation; justify your behavior; retaliate; find ways to contain and ameliorate your upset.

Your immediate, knee-jerk response is unlikely to be a calm consideration of the response options available to you, nor are you likely in the heat of the moment to thoughtfully consider how to modify your behavior in order to avoid such a situation in the future.

The child or adolescent faced with an emotionally charged parental reaction is most likely to focus on how mean or unfair it is for the parent to go on and on about the child's behavior—behavior the child finds easy to rationalize. It is usually most effective for the parent to keep whatever needs to be said brief, to the point, and with appropriately intense emotion. It is not necessary to say it more than once.

With adolescents, it is often most effective for the parent to keep his emotional reaction to the young person's behavior completely in check. This leaves the adolescent with nothing to focus on but his own behavior.

For example, my husband and I went away for the weekend, leaving our two, generally quite responsible teenagers to take care of the family dog. I called home on Saturday night and the *dog* answered the telephone! Our kids had evidently left the phone, which had a long cord, on the floor. At the moment the telephone rang, the dog heard something outside and knocked the receiver off the base of the telephone as she ran, barking, to the front door.

I repeatedly tried to call home for the next two hours but got only a busy signal. Eventually I reached a friend who was willing to climb into the house through an upstairs window, let the dog out, and hang up the phone.

Clearly the kids had not been at home as promised. When we returned home we decided not the give the kids a chance to focus on our intense negative reaction to their dereliction of duty. In deadly calm voices, we told them about the dog answering the phone, which proved they had not been home. We told them that the fun activities in their lives were at a standstill until they presented us with what we would consider an appropriate consequence. We then left the room, relieved at having avoided a draining confrontation. Before long they presented us with a suitable consequence. No one in the family can remember what the consequence was. However, when reminded of the incident several years later, when the kids were in their early twenties, they said that refraining from visiting our anger on them in a lengthy tirade was extremely effective in depriving them of opportunity to complain about their parents' "unreasonable" rage, and helped them focus more quickly on a consequence acceptable to us.

Problems with using Time-Out: It can be unproductive and/or too disturbing for some children. If this is the case with your child, you might try lightening up a bit and redefining time-out as a short period of time during which the child is without a favored toy.

When utilizing time-out, remember that if it exceeds the child's grasp of time, she may forget the why she was placed in time-out. For a two-year-old, five minutes may be an eternity, causing the child to believe he has been abandoned forever. Abandonment becomes the child's sole focus. The reason the child was put in time-out is forgotten. As a general rule, think of one minute of time-out for every year of life. Two minutes for a two-year-old is likely to be sufficient for time-out or toy deprivation.

If the time-out location is attractive enough, the child may not mind spending time there, so take care to choose an unappealing place for time-out. If the child is younger than seven years old, and the time-out location does not provide opportunity for the child to physically express her upset, those feelings may continue to dominate the child's mood after time-out has been completed. She may be told she can come out of time-out after the parent sees some of her upset energy coming out (for example, by pounding the bed mattress, or by kicking or tearing a cardboard carton into pieces and throwing the pieces into a trash can).

It is helpful to tell some children that time-out will be over at the point when the child is sure the parent won't see the offending behavior again for a long time. After spending only three minutes in time-out, four-year-old Raylene wanted out. She told her father that he wouldn't hear her scream at her two-year-old sister for a long time. Within two minutes of her return to the living room, her father was again subjected to Raylene's loud screaming at her sister. At that point her father said, "Raylene, *you* had a chance to decide when time-out should end, and that didn't work out very well. So *I* am going to put you back in time-out, and this time *I* will decide when time-out should end."

Inevitably, any child will at times behave in ways that are unacceptable to the parent, resulting in an encounter that is unpleasant for both child and parent. When calm has been restored after such an upset, the parent can ask whether or not the child understands what the parent found unacceptable.

Once the unacceptable behavior is identified and understood by both child and parent, the parent can say, "So instead of what just happened, next time, I want you to …" and allow the child to complete the sentence. When the child finds a suitable alternative and employs it, the parent should praise the child.

## Special Time

The child must follow adult plans and behavioral rules during the majority of the child's waking hours. Possibly the most important action the parent can take in the interest of gaining behavioral compliance from the child is to implement regularly occurring Special Time with each child (including adolescents) in the family.

During Special Time, roles of parent and child are reversed—i.e. the child becomes ruler of the realm. This makes parental behavioral requirements more acceptable to the child at other times. For example, the parent can say, "We are in the supermarket right now and I am in charge; you will be in charge this afternoon, during Special Time."

Special Time is scheduled time during which one adult spends time in a room with one child, following the lead of the child in chosen activities (within the bounds of house rules and safety concerns) or discussed topics. No electronic devices are to be used during this time by either child or adult, and no interruptions by other family members are permitted.

Beyond enforcing limits concerning safety and household rules (such as putting one game away before taking out another), the parent makes no suggestions about how the activity is to be conducted and participates in it only in response to instructions given by the child. For example, if the child decides to rearrange furniture in the doll house, the parent is attentive to the child but does nothing he or she is not instructed to do. Parent and child can chat as the project unfolds, but the choice of topics belongs to the child.

The parent seeks to convey an abiding interest in the child himself, not in a particular activity chosen by the child. If both parent and child love playing chess, the child may not understand that the parent's primary interest is in the child, and not in chess.

Nancy repeatedly chose a board game to play that involved only chance, a game she knew her parent did not enjoy. After five such Special Times during which the parent cheerfully played the game, Nancy, reassured that the parent's interest was in being with Nancy herself, chose other activities.

Having a child accompany you as you drive somewhere can be enjoyable for both of you, but the child is not in charge during the drive. Looking at a screen together (TV, computer, movie) can also be an enjoyable, shared activity, but in that situation, the focus is on the screen and not on each other—so it is wise to set a no-screen rule for Special Time.

Special Time is most effective when it occurs at a time during which the parent could be spending time with more than just one child. Help from the other parent or another adult is needed if other children in the household are too young to entertain themselves—however even kindergarten-aged children can gradually learn to entertain themselves for at least thirty minutes. Most parents report that their children so enjoy being chosen for Special Time, that after two rotations of Special Time with all children in the household, there will be no interruptions.

If no other adults are available to help, and Special Time with a child under kindergarten age can only occur when a baby sibling is asleep, it is helpful to have the child observe the parent *explaining* to the baby that he will have to stay in his crib and nap since it is the parent's turn to have Special Time with the older child.

A parent annoyed with the child's behavior prior to the scheduled Special Time may well be tempted to cancel it. The parent needs to remember that Special Time is for the parent, NOT for the child. The child can be told, "If I don't have Special Time with you today (or this week, if there is a rotation of Special Time between all children in the family), then I will miss the time to know who you are now. By tomorrow (or next week), you will be older, and you may have changed."

An adolescent is often less than enthusiastic about spending time with a parent. An exception to the no screen rule may be needed. Seeing a movie or video, even playing a video game together, along with eating some favorite food before or after the screen activity, may be beneficial. In this instance Special Time occurs during the eating, as long as what is talked about is chosen by the adolescent. Again, what is crucial is following the adolescent's lead in the conversation. It is never a time to correct the adolescent's behavior or ideas, or share your adult wisdom, unless specifically asked to do so.

If the adolescent shows little interest in talking at all, practice being patient in silence. This conveys that you sincerely mean to follow the young person's lead during Special Time. Fifteen-year-old Randy's father told me that Randy only started to talk with him after four silent Special Times.

Family lives are complicated, and as children get older, children and adults need to collaborate to schedule Special Time. However, once it's on the calendar, cancellations by either party should be rare, and a replacement time should be agreed upon at the time of the cancellation, and adhered to.

## Child's Play Is Child's Work

Many adults view playtime as nothing more than the way children occupy themselves until they get old enough to participate in legitimate learning and academic skill-building activities. In fact, this is far from the truth. Play is the way that children learn about themselves and about the world. The work of Jean Piaget and many other researchers demonstrates that from birth the child is compelled from within, programmed to use his physical, cognitive and emotional energy to interact with objects and people, becoming increasingly effective in influencing his environment.

The infant and growing child pursue pleasure, knowledge, and skill through use of their inborn interest in what is new and different and by repeating experiences that are already familiar. Think of your own experience—once you learned how to swim and found it enjoyable, you probably wished to continue to swim. Parents often rush a child on towards mastering new competencies without regard for the fact that the child enjoys repeating what he has already mastered. The pleasure he derives from using the already mastered skills will, in fact, motivate him to increase his skill in other areas later on. We see a clear example of this when a child wants his parent to read his favorite book to him over and over, along with a vast number of new books.

Through her play, a child is in effect conducting a continuing stream of experiments. These experiments are essential activities for the acquisition of important life skills. For example: "Will this rubber doll make the same sound as the plastic set of keys when I drop them out of my crib? What does that chair leg taste like? Will the crayon fit in my nostril? What will happen if I say 'No' to my mother?"

Play is the primary method the infant and very young child use to gather and organize impressions. This is why it is essential to provide a variety of opportunities and materials with which to experiment, i.e. play. The infant or young child does not yet have words for what she is learning so it is also important to expose her to as much verbal language as possible.

Martha, in her highchair, accidentally pushes her bowl of peas onto the floor. Her startled mother exclaims, "Uh oh!" while chasing down the scattered peas on the kitchen floor. Martha finds the entire process entertaining! She soon discovers that she can purposefully push her bowl of food so that it falls onto the floor. Her mother again exclaims, leans down and cleans up the mess. Martha discovers foods of different shapes and colors make different patterns on the floor. and elicit different responses from her mother. Martha tries to both replicate and invent new forms of this interesting chain of events again, and again, and again.

It is messy and annoying for Martha's mother, but Martha is learning many new things, including, on a physical level, the meaning of *let go*, *push*, and *fall*. As Martha experiments, she also learns that her actions produce interesting responses from her mother. The repeating sequence of Martha pushing the bowl off her highchair tray, her mother exclaiming, picking up and replacing on Martha's tray the bowl and food (drop the spoon, spoon is picked up and replaced, spoon is dropped, etc.) is in fact a real conversation (another important concept for the child to learn), conducted on a physical level between Martha and her mother.

Eighteen-month-old Alejandro experimented with speed, seeing how fast he could run away from his father in a crowded mall. Alejandro's father, for safety reasons, stopped the experiment at the mall after only a single trial. Alejandro's experiments with speed at home, as he tried to run his train around the circular train track at high speed, were longer-lasting and more enlightening.

Pushing the train at high speed around the track caused the train to derail. Each time this happened, Alejandro said out loud to himself, "Otra vez" (again!), and returned the train cars to the track and tried again. After a number of failed attempts he discovered that a moderate speed was the only way to have the train successfully move all the way around the track. He was also practicing labeling the physical action he was taking with words he had heard his parents use.

Four-year-old Yvonne's nursery school teacher watched her "dress up" in style for a grand imaginary occasion. She wore a large, floppy hat, high heels, a sequined dress, a shawl and carried an enormous pocket book in the crook of her arm. She scooped up an assortment of items from a nearby shelf and dropped them into the pocketbook. She briefly studied the contents, then removed some of the items and replaced them with other objects. She did this several times, each time noting the contents of the pocketbook with some dissatisfaction. Finally, she peered into the pocketbook and announced, "There, that's the right amount of stuff!" She snapped the pocketbook closed and teetered off on her high heels.

Not until the teacher heard Yvonne's statement did she realize that Yvonne's activity with the pocketbook was an experiment in mathematical estimating. It was likely that Yvonne, repeatedly watching her mother load and unload her pocketbook with "stuff," had concluded that the aim was to fill it with the correct *amount* of "stuff" (the idea that her mother was trying to get the *appropriate* "stuff" into her pocketbook was still beyond Yvonne's awareness).

In addition to providing opportunities to learn important concepts, play allows the young child to take risks—and to make mistakes—without dire consequence. Seeing what happens when different colors of play dough are mixed together is much less problematic for parents than mixing white milk with red cranberry juice, although the child may see the two as equally interesting color-mixing, cause-and-effect experiments.

If judgment of a child's finished playtime project is left to the child himself ("What do *you* think about the block building you just made?"), he is more likely to risk investing emotionally and intellectually in further projects, and is more likely to see himself as a competent individual with good ideas and skills, and to be willing to take risks in kindergarten and in subsequent grades in school.

Play with other children also provides opportunities to practice and increase her ability to express and communicate effectively, and to negotiate and resolve conflicts cooperatively. For example, three-year-olds Jillian and Nancy were playing house in the nursery school loft. "We have *hot* water in the house," announced Nancy. "No, we have *cold* water in the house," retorted Jillian.

The two children locked gazes for a long minute. Nancy looked as though she might cry. "Okay," Nancy finally said, "You have cold water in the house, and I have hot water in the house." The two went happily back to playing—play that allowed them opportunities to practice skills they will need when, as adults, they manage and share real households with others.

In play, the child can change one or more aspects of reality—for instance, changing his experience from being passive to playing an active role in what occurs. The day after receiving a painful injection, a child during play, may take on the role of the doctor, delivering a painful injection to the child's stuffed pony. "I'm sorry, but you have to have this injection and it's going to hurt a lot," the child doctor tells the pony. After delivering the shot, the child switches to play the role of mother, comforting the pony.

In play, the young child can enjoy a pleasure that may no longer be compatible with his sense of dignity. For instance, a four-year-old playing with his kindergarten peers can opt to be the baby in a pretend family. Or, he can "play baby" with his parent, letting himself be wrapped up in a blanket, sitting on his parent's lap in the rocking chair where his mother frequently sits, rocks, and nurses the new baby.

A wise parent is careful when commenting on what the young child creates during play time. What appears to be a meaningless scribble to an adult may seem a clearly drawn fish to the young artist. A young child believes the adults in her life know what she is thinking. If the parent asks, "What is it?" the child is confused by the parent's inability to perceive the fish. She is also saddened that her attempt to communicate "fish" to the parent has failed.

## A Child's Artwork – Significant Stages of Development and Appropriate Parental Response

The physical ability to manipulate art materials isn't developed until about eighteen months of age. Therefore, art materials made available to the child generally end up in his or her mouth rather than in an artistic product. For this reason, art supplies are not generally recommended for children under eighteen months.

There is one happy exception. Let the child finger paint with edible puddings, or "sculpt" with chunks of gelatin dessert on the high chair tray or a washable placemat. Suggestions for art activities appropriate for children of different ages are included elsewhere in this writing.

The young child's artwork is an expression of how he is thinking and feeling. It is also an attempt to communicate something to the observer or recipient of the artwork. For example, in one school, each kindergarten student drew a picture of his family. These pictures were used to decorate the classroom for parents' night.

Brian's parents were upset that his depiction of his pet rabbit dwarfed those of the human family members. The parents feared this indicated that Brian's parents and siblings were not important to Brian. They were relieved when the teacher suggested that the picture more probably indicated Brian's happiness at receiving a pet rabbit as a gift for his recent birthday—a pet rabbit had been at the top of his wish list for a long time.

As emphasized elsewhere in this writing, the child under seven or eight years of age views his creative actions and products as parts of himself, exposed to the world. The child perceives negative comments about his artwork as judgmental or dismissive of his essential self—who he is at the core. Comments like "What is it? That's not what color clouds are!" or "That looks more like a dog than a lion," are hurtful. By contrast, it is fine to indicate what parts of his artwork you particularly like. Ask the child which part of his work *he* likes the most, or simply ask him to tell you about what he has drawn or made. Asking a child to tell you about art he has created—or even, for example, something he has built ("That green part of the vehicle you have built from plastic blocks looks interesting; tell me about it.") builds the child's self-esteem because it positions the child as the expert, capable of informing his less knowledgeable parent. If the child proclaims that he doesn't like his artwork or that it isn't any good, it is fine to say that you and he have different ideas about his work—that although he doesn't seem to be happy with it, you enjoy looking at it. It is important to keep firmly in mind that the artist is the only expert where his artwork is concerned. Only he has the right to pronounce any negative judgment on it and only he knows exactly what it means. For example, four-year-old Bethany drew a picture of herself and her two parents. Her father, who appeared to be holding Bethany in his arms, occupied most of the paper space. Bethany's mother had been drawn off to one side lying down. She was larger than Bethany but much smaller than Bethany's father. Inside the mother's protruding, much scribbled around belly was a drawing of a baby. A close look at Bethany's drawing of herself revealed a circle on top of Bethany's belly. Inside the circle she had drawn a tiny, four-legged animal.

In fact, Bethany's father had replaced his wife as Bethany's primary caretaker two months previously, when his wife had been put on bed rest for the remainder of her pregnancy. When asked by her teacher to tell something about her drawing, Bethany promptly and cheerfully identified her father, her mother, and herself. Pointing to the drawing of the baby inside her mother's belly, she proudly announced that her mother was a grown up and was going to have a baby. Then, pointing to the creature drawn on her own belly, she explained that since she was a child, and small, she was going to have a hamster.

## The First Stage of Art Development
### (eighteen to thirty-six months of age)

This stage begins with disorganized horizontal and vertical scribbles that the child makes by moving his arm across the page in an outward motion arc from elbow to hand, while holding a drawing implement in his hand. It is helpful to let the child use paper large enough for the entire arc.

Horizontal and vertical lines are followed by circular scribbles. As the child recognizes that he can choose to start or stop a line, and make it here or there, he begins to draw within the boundary of the paper. These scribbled drawings are made, named, and then re-named. They may be given to one person, and a bit later, they may be repossessed by the child, and given to someone else.

Eventually the child learns to draw a closed circle. A plan for drawing both the human figure and a few objects develops. These plans, or schemas, remain constant for many months. The circle represents both head and body. Some facial features, along with hair may be added within the circle. Lines indicating arms and legs extend outward from the closed circle.

Parents may give children of this age a small paintbrush with a small container of water to take outside where they can change the light-dark value of objects in the yard. This age group also enjoys finger painting on paper. Edible finger paints (puddings, for instance) on washable placemats or plastic plates can be especially fun. Letting children use their hands to make play dough or mix cookie dough delights them and also increases hand strength. These kinds of pleasurable, mess-making experiences increase children's tolerance for *messing up* academically when they are older. Recipes for creating pretzels and gingerbread men cookies (the dough serves as an excellent sculpting clay) are included elsewhere in this writing.

It is important to remember that children are most interested in the process of creating, which is to them an important way of expressing and communicating. Once a child has *said* what he wants to say (he is done with the picture), he turns his attention to the next *to-do*, no longer much interested in the product he has just completed. By sharp contrast, the finished product is often the adult's sole, or primary interest.

## The Second Stage of Art Development
### (three to five years of age)

During this stage the child develops his own way of representing the human form. An enclosed form indicating the human body is added to the single circle that previously represented both head and body. Arms and legs extend out from the newly added body circle. Facial features occur more regularly, and in more detail. Eyes, ears, mouth, and nose area are added and indicate increased awareness of the senses. Rather than occurring all over the paper, objects are placed on what is referred to as a ground line.

More than one object is drawn or painted on a single sheet of paper, and the objects are separate from each other, but may be related thematically to each other. For instance, two zoo animals, or a house and a person may be depicted in the same scene. Colors are used, but their use is not reality based.

Time, in relation to changes and sequences of events, is of great interest to the child during this developmental stage. Mixing dough (bread, gingerbread, pretzel or play dough) supports this interest. Ingredients are added in order, combined, possibly cooked for a time, after which the child can experiment with, or consume the final product. She can experiment with making changes in the size, density, and shapes of what she sculpts.

Fat, easy-to-grip crayons require more focus and force to use than magic markers and increase the child's ability to control what she is drawing. However, she enjoys and can manage a variety of art materials, including magic markers, glue, various types of tape, paints and easel, and eventually scissors.

## The Third Stage of Art Development
### (six to nine or ten years of age, or up to the onset of puberty)

By first grade, children can draw pictures containing a number of objects arranged in definite relationship to each other. There may be a house and a person standing outside under a tree, while the sun shines from above. Or there may be a school bus, with children in the playground outside of a school. Rows of objects—flowers for instance—appear, along with rainbows. People are generally drawn as smaller than houses but larger than flowers, indicating increasing awareness of the actual relative size of objects and people.

The child's interest and ability in realistically representing people and objects increases. He develops the skill to draw with true perspective. Multiple ground lines in his pictures indicate differences in terrain and distinguish near, middle, and far away space. In one painting there may be people in a tent in the foreground with a lake clearly at some distance behind the tent, while on the other side of the lake mountains rise to touch the clouds.

Around the same time children develop the ability to use abstract thinking, they begin to assess their own artistic ability relative to the ability of others. Their interest in creating art—or their aversion to it (and this can be strong) depends on whether or not the child and significant others in his life perceive that he possesses artistic ability.

### The Fourth Stage of Art Development
(puberty through adolescence)

The adolescent who identifies herself as possessing artistic ability is likely to pursue all sorts of art-related activities. The child who thinks she lacks such ability will avoid it at all costs. Regardless of self-perceived artistic ability, almost all adolescents will strenuously resist being asked to draw a full human figure. The vast and unsettling physical, cognitive, and emotional changes they are experiencing seem to result in a strong desire not to acknowledge, at least on paper, what might be going on below the neck.

Adolescents are also often reluctant to draw with colors. Some theorists correlate use of colors with how comfortable an adolescent is with his or her own intense and constant changing feelings. The adolescent may avoid committing emotion-laden colors to paper where they are available for others to see and comment on them.

## Sharing Literature With the Child – Story Books, Fables, Myths, and Old-Fashioned Fairy Tales

Child development theorists and educators agree that the child's development in general, and language ability in particular, is greatly advanced by exposure to spoken and written language. The more words the child is exposed to, the better. Talking with the tiniest infant, by exchanging sounds, is very important. Reading and talking about books with children who can read on their own hones language comprehension skills far beyond their reading levels.

Consulting other parents or a librarian in the children's books section—or visiting a book store specializing in good children's literature—can be extremely helpful in determining which books to share with your child. There are many ways to enhance the experience of reading to a child.

## Literary To-Dos

Reading a picture book designed for toddlers who lack verbal skills can link words the toddler hears with images he sees. When, for example, a fourteen-month-old who has repeatedly been read to from the same book is asked, "Where is the ball?" he may be able to point to the appropriate picture. If asked, "Was the little bird sad when he couldn't find his mother?" the toddler can nod his head affirmatively. If this shared *reading* experience is enjoyable, it lays the groundwork for the idea that conversation and *book learning* can be fun.

When reading with a young child, ask questions: "How does this character feel? What do you think he will do next? What do you think will happen next? What do you think will happen after that?" It is very important to accept whatever ideas the child expresses, and to refrain from a discussion of whether they are credible or not. You can ask the child, "Tell me more about why you think that will happen," or "Let's read on and find out."

Children love to hear the same story many times over, and often memorize it word by word. Try leaving out the last word in a sentence in a Dr. Seuss book—or any rhyming book. Chances are the child will supply it. Remember to read with expression and at a pace appropriate to the child's ability to absorb what he is hearing.

Videotapes of children's books cannot offer an experience comparable to the experience a child has when sitting with a parent who demonstrates by his behavior that he and the child are united when sharing this enjoyable activity. Words and actions in almost all videos proceed faster than the young child's ability to digest them.

Reading dialogue aloud and acting out well known stories, such as *The Gingerbread Boy* or *Goldilocks and the Three Bears*, can be great fun for both children and adults.

Try making a version of something that was used by characters in a well-known story. For instance, make a canoe out of stiff paper and sail it in the bathtub or sink, recalling the adventures of the main character in E. B. White's book, *Stuart Little*. Have a "wild rumpus" in which the child is permitted to jump on the bed or run about shrieking for a few minutes, like Max in Richard Scary's book, *Where The Wild Things Are*. Bake dough figures from *The Gingerbread Boy* and decorate them.

Try telling a well-loved story with the child during an unexpected delay that might otherwise be considered wasted time, such as at the doctor's office, or an extended traffic jam.

Create a lively group activity by making up a story with one or several children. The most basic story has three parts: a main character—the character has a problem—the problem is solved. The plot of the story unfolds as the main character takes the steps necessary to address and ultimately resolve the problem. The first child can say who the character is, the second identifies the problem, the third child solves the problem. This very basic story can be endlessly expanded. For instance, "Tell something about the character. Were there any other characters? Did the problem get worse before it got better? What solutions were tried that didn't work?" Using the analogy of drawing may encourage more description and detail in the stories. Point out that a drawing with pen or pencil may be interesting, but that if colors are added to the drawing, it often becomes much more so. Telling a story with descriptive words is like painting with colors.

If the parent records the story on a tape recorder or writes it down on paper as the child tells it, the *writers* of the story can enjoy hearing it over and over. This lays the foundation for the child to see him or herself as a competent writer.

Children who have difficulty writing and/or reading have particular difficulty seeing themselves as authors. Print the stories. The children may illustrate them if they wish. These original *books* can be given as gifts to important people in the child's life.

*Aesop's Fables*, like others of that genre, have universal appeal because they depict universal predicaments. However, fables are cautionary tales that deliver moral instructions. There are no hidden meanings and the consequences of bad behavior are spelled out. They are unlike fairy tales, which set the child up to try to find his own solutions to universal dilemmas.

Myths can be majestic, tragic, or pessimistic and, like fables, are meant to move readers and listeners to do the *morally correct* thing. They are set in faraway and fantastic places and involve improbable events and divine beings who behave in ways human beings never could. Myths are aimed at helping adults come to grips with being alone and with death. Exposing children to myths is not appropriate until they are at least nine or ten years of age.

Old-fashioned fairy tales, unlike fables and myths, foster the young child's development. In recent years there has been a trend towards *sanitizing* traditional fairy tales like *Cinderella, Hansel and Gretel, The Three Little Pigs*, and *Little Red Riding Hood*. The probable intention is to protect young children from being frightened. However, fairy tales are actually reassuring to the child because they bear a striking resemblance to the young child's interior life (the way they think and feel about people and events).

Characters in fairy tales perform amazing feats and experience dramatic transformations, just like those experienced daily by the young child. Remember that four-year-olds live with family members who, when angry, may strongly resemble powerful, carnivorous dinosaurs. Children often need flashlights with which to fend off the monsters they vividly imagine living under their beds at night.

In like manner, the adults in children's lives seem to possess magical powers—in minutes a perfect Super Hero costume emerges from Mom's sewing machine, and Grandmother serves ice cream for breakfast at her house. Miraculous and sudden metamorphoses occur. For example, Mother, who closely resembles the loved grandmother in *Little Red Riding Hood* when playing with the child, can instantly change into the hated wolf in Grandmother's nightgown when she puts the child in bed for a nap. The mother resumes her beloved status when she returns to wake the child with a hug after the nap the child didn't want to take.

The parent may have dulled awareness of his or her own intensely negative and positive thoughts and feelings, and can manage them in the light of reality. However, the young child is all too aware of his own intensely felt feelings. He may struggle daily with how to deal with them. In addition, until he reaches puberty, he cannot experience intense emotions without immediately acting on them, or wishing to do so.

Characters in fairy tales regularly act on intense positive and negative feelings that the child herself regularly experiences. Identifying with the protagonist in fairy tales gives the child hope that she will be able to succeed in integrating, modifying, and moderating these thoughts and feelings in her own daily life.

The protagonists in traditional fairy tales must grapple with situations with which the child will have to grapple: The three pigs must leave their mother's house and make their own way in the world. Little Red Riding Hood must discharge the duty of traveling through the dark woods to deliver a basket of food to her ailing grandmother.

The protagonists encounter difficulties which they, with the help of adult characters, are able to resolve. The three pigs must construct houses for themselves. Little Red Riding Hood encounters a wolf in her grandmother's bed. Most importantly, the only characters experiencing negative consequences for their actions are adults. In spite of intense feelings, and initially overwhelming circumstances, no harm ever comes to the young protagonists in fairy tales.

Finally, fairy tales take place long ago, often involve animals, and take place far from where the child sits with his parent listening to the story.

## Productive Problem-Solving Discussions and Role Modeling for Parents

A great deal of what the young child observes when his adult family members interact with each other is incorporated into the child's long-term ideas about how relationships are to be conducted. Therefore, possible ways to model effective resolution (re-solution) of the disagreements that are an inevitable part of all significant and ongoing adult relationships must be considered.

As early in the parents' relationship with each other as possible, they should try to establish ground rules for how disagreements are to be handled. Ron and Wendy used a system that many couples find helpful. If a disagreement becomame too upsetting (for whatever reason) to either partner, that person could call a time-out and put the discussion temporarily on hold.

If Wendy called a time-out, it was her responsibility to get back to Ron within an hour, either to signal that she was ready to resume the discussion or to announce that she needed more time. She was also responsible for scheduling a continuation of the discussion as soon as possible. When the discussion resumed, only the original issue was addressed, not who had wanted time-out and why.

When one or both partners are too intensely upset to discuss an issue, a five-minute venting session about the issue, (not the *partner*), is sometimes useful. While venting, each partner can say anything he or she is thinking or feeling or wanting to have or not to have happen with two exceptions:

The word *you* cannot be used. As discussed previously, this word is universally heard as a personal attack. This is almost impossible to do when emotions are running high—almost inevitably, one partner will use this word. If Ron, for instance, uses the word *you* when venting about Wendy, she can say, in a neutral tone, "I heard the word *you*." This gives Ron a chance to repeat his complaint, but this time without the inflammatory *you* word.

After a venting session, some time may be needed for each partner to digest what was said and heard and to think about how to best approach the upcoming discussion on the subject.

Try to schedule a discussion as soon after an upsetting event as possible. Do not deny that you were in fact upset. Do not try to not let it bother you, because "it really wasn't important enough to mention or to get upset about." Do not make the assumption that you won't be listened to anyway, so why bother to even try to talk about it.

There is an expression that says, "I'll tell you now or I'll get you later." Feelings of upset very rarely simply go away. If not acknowledged and dealt with, they will resurface and trip us up later. One unacknowledged or never-addressed upset on top of another builds and builds to an inevitable crisis. The explosion may or may not be related to the original upset, which is often relatively insignificant to the size and intensity of the explosion. By the time the explosion occurs there's a big and complicated mess to clean up.

When an upset occurs, it's beneficial for each partner to identify the most recent time that each was feeling all right about the way things were going between them. For example: "We were getting along okay at lunch, but by dinner time I was furious."

Next, try to pinpoint the first upsetting thing—in other words, the transition between the time when things were okay and when they weren't (in our example, between lunch and dinner). Then discuss and try to re-solve that first upset ONLY. The first upset usually fuels each subsequent upset, so it's usually best to let all of the subsequent upsets between lunch and dinner go undiscussed for the time being.

If, when you previously tried to discuss a concern, emotions rose above intense conversational level, or if you fear that there will be some unhappy and unproductive escalation, try to hold the discussion in a location that will encourage, and even enforce, good behavior on the part of both partners—a library, restaurant, or hotel lobby, for instance. This can be helpful for separated or divorced parents with an acrimonious relationship who must regularly meet to discuss arrangements involving their children.

Utilize reflective listening, saying back to your partner what you have understood him or her to have said. This is effective in clearing up misunderstandings, and also conveys that attention is being paid to the speaker and his or her message.

Keep references to traits and behaviors that appear to you to be shared by your partner and one or more members of his or her family or origin out of the discussion. We all have deeply held feelings about members of our families of origin and our possible behavioral resemblances to them. Defensive or attacking reactions are extremely likely to follow a partner's reference to such resemblances. For example, saying "I often feel you are not listening to me" will be better received by a partner than saying "You are a bad listener just like your mother and your brother!"

It's best to discuss one topic during a single discussion, even though there are almost always a number of closely related and relevant topics. It is also best to discuss one level of dissatisfaction at a time. For example: overall dissatisfaction with the way a relationship has been going for the past three months is one level; dissatisfaction with how poorly the bathroom has been cleaned during the past three months is quite a different level.

A discussion should begin with each partner stating the topic of his concern and his or her desired result of the discussion. Most importantly, this discussion should include from each partner a suggestion for a solution of the problem. For example: "I have zero free time for myself and yet I'm being told that I'm selfish and that I don't care about spending time with the family. I want time for each of us away from the family at least once a week. I'd like Saturday afternoons for myself."

Beginning this way can lead to a short discussion with satisfactory results. If the partner agrees with the proposed solution, the discussion is over. If the partner doesn't agree, he or she should either state what modifications would make the proposal acceptable, or else propose a different solution. The discussion continues until the couple comes up with a plan with which both can agree.

A true problem solving discussion involves both partners working together to find an acceptable solution, not attacking each other's ideas, or worse, attacking who the other person is. A problem solving discussion is over when both partners agree to make and continue a behavioral change for an agreed upon period of time. This resolution includes setting a time and place at the end of the stated period to get together to evaluate and discuss the effect of the agreed on changes.

Each partner needs to follow through with what he or she has agreed to do, regardless of whether or not he or she believes the partner has done likewise. Coming to that second discussion saying, "Well, my partner stopped doing his/her part, so I stopped doing mine," is a recipe for failure, and erodes hope for the success of future discussions and agreements.

Stay in the present when stating a concern. Going back into the past is never going to be helpful, even if the concern has been long standing. For instance, "I no longer want to have to remind my partner to take out the trash" is likely to be more effective than saying "I've never gotten the help I've wanted with taking the trash out, and I'm sick of it."

Only true "I" statements are to be made. There is widespread misunderstanding about what "I" statements are and are not. For example: "I was really angry when you insulted me at my friend's house" is not an "I" statement because it contains the word "you," and thus an accusation about the other person's behavior along with an implication about the intention behind that person's behavior.

Saying "I felt really angry at my friend's house, when I heard what to me sounded like a real insult" IS an "I" statement because it refers only to the speaker's experience. Reference to what the other partner did or intended is strictly avoided. Use of sarcasm should be banned from any discussion. It is important to remember that sarcasm is in the *ear* of the listener, not in the *perception* of the speaker.

## Top Tips to Help Parents and Children Get Along With Each Other

1. Express Appreciation for the Child's Positive Actions: Catch your child when he is being successful, kind, or responsible, or when he has made a good decision. Be specific about the action taken by the child that was particularly pleasing to you rather than making a global comment about the child, such as "You're wonderful."

2. Family Rules: Three simple rules should be consistently applied. These will address a wide range of unwanted behaviors:

    - People and animals have feelings, so physical hurting and verbal hurting of feelings (put downs) are not allowed. There will be a consequence for both.

    - Children must put things they have finished playing with back in their proper places before moving on to another activity, or leaving the area of the first activity.

    - Another's belongings cannot be borrowed without prior permission from the owner. In addition, the owner's refusal to lend his belongings must be accepted.

    It is important to remember that the vast majority of the young child's time is spent following the lead of an adult, who alone determines what, how, and when things are to happen. Having regularly occurring Special Time with each child in the family greatly increases the child's willingness to follow adult leadership at other times and provides ongoing proof of the esteemed position the child holds in the parent's life and heart.

3. Telling True Stories: Tell your children stories about your own growing up years. Most of the stories should involve how you landed in, and/or contributed to, unfortunate situations. Books and stories in which happiness and good fortune surround the lives of all characters are far less interesting than those in which difficulties abound.

4. Sharing: Try sharing "the best thing that happened today" and "the yuckiest thing that happened today" stories with your children during dinnertime. This encourages more information being shared than simply asking "What did you do today?" The focus should be on how the individual felt (happy, sad, angry, scared) about events, not recitation of the events themselves.

5. Advance Notice: Let the child know what behavior will, and will not, be acceptable prior to entering a situation that might be problematic for the child. With older children, some prior negotiation about this can prevent upset feelings later. Parents tend to tell children only what behavior is *not* permitted. Make it clear whose rules apply if more than one adult in a position of authority will be present. The child doesn't find it difficult to accept that Grandmother and Father have different behavioral requirements for him, even if both adults are in the room with the child. The child just needs to be told which adult is in charge of the child's behavior on a particular occasion.

6. The Blob and the Wild Moment Pillow: The Blob can be a giant pillow made of three and one-half yards of sixty-inch wide, seamless cotton T-shirt jersey. Knot one end of the jersey. Fill it with the equivalent of a middle density, full-sized, four-inch thick foam mattress that has been cut into four-inch cubes. Knot the other end of the jersey. When desired, one end can be unknotted to dump out the cubes, which can then be used to construct buildings, towers, and forts large enough for the child to crawl into. The constructions do no harm and make no noise when they come tumbling down. An upholsterer may be willing to cut the mattress into four-inch cubes. If you decide to cut the cubes yourself, never do it on a rug or carpet (shreds will never come out). Use an electric knife or a serrated bread knife.

The Blob may also be made out of a rectangle of fake fur or fleece large enough to envelop the child's entire body. Sew up the sides but install a twelve-inch zipper opening through which the cubes can come and go.

The Wild Moment Pillow is a king size pillow with a distinctive pillow case. The pillow can be used during moments of wildness! The young child learns by doing. He learns that it is okay to express feelings physically in appropriate settings. It is most helpful if the adults model venting on such a pillow on occasion, for their own adult upsets. For example, "I was really upset because I had a flat tire on the way to work today, but I stomped on The Wild Moment Pillow three times, and now I feel better."

7. Safe Place for a Wild Moment: Attempting to reason with an emotional and upset person rarely works out well. Ignoring an upset child having a meltdown in the room where adults are trying to talk doesn't work for either generation. Putting the child on the Blob—or in a safe, (and boring) place—until relative calm is restored is a wise option.

8. Work It Out Yourselves: It is most unlikely that children of different ages, or children who are very upset with each other, will be able to resolve a problem between them without the active presence of an adult. Tell the children to try to resolve the problem with words—but that if this doesn't work, it is their job to let the adult in charge know about the problem before any physical action is taken by anyone involved in the dispute.

    An adult should be available to lend aid if requested. Often just being present while the children negotiate is enough. Don't forget to outlaw use of the word *you*. Letting each child punctuate the points he is trying to make by poking or punching the Blob may help defuse the situation.

9. The Word *You*: Remember that "you" is a fine word to use when pleased with what someone has done. It is never a helpful word when you are displeased with someone's behavior. Minus that word, disputants can only speak about what each experienced and how each felt about what impacted him or her. For example: "You took my sweater, I hate you" becomes "My sweater was taken, and I hate it when my things are taken!" Re-solution of the difficulty becomes more likely because no verbal attacks can be launched in the absence of the word *you*.

# Preparing for the Arrival of a New Baby

Life is completely different when one child is added to a couple's life. Equally significant and pervasive differences result from the addition of each additional child to family life. While parents may happily welcome a new family member, children of two to six years of age will not necessarily share their parents' enthusiasm. Opportunities to share thoughts and feelings about the new family member, both positive and negative, should be provided.

For example, three-year-old Anna was getting ready to go to the hospital to meet her new baby sister for the first time. Anna happily explained to her grandmother that "When the new baby comes home, she is going to come home with a new mother."

Three-year-old Jack was happily baking cookies with his mother while his father looked after the new baby in another room. Jack was looking forward to eating the cookies. He looked up at his mother and happily asked, "Can't we cook the baby and eat him too?"

Four-year-old Helen, speaking with her mother on the telephone after the mother had given birth to the fourth younger brother, exclaimed, "You stay in the hospital until you get a girl!" Helen had been hoping for a sister to begin to even things up.

Five-year-old Becky's kindergarten class was discussing a recent trip they had taken to a farm. The children had been particularly impressed by a mother pig and her eleven piglets. The teacher reminded them that one of the piglets was a runt and she asked the group if anyone knew what a runt was. Becky immediately raised her hand and offered, "A runt is the one that is smaller than all the rest, and nobody wants it."

"You have a runt at your house, don't you," her teacher commented.

"Yes, replied Becky, my new baby brother, Michael."

Ask the older child comparative questions about his feelings regarding the new family member. For example: "How high are you happy/angry that the new brother is here? Up to the table, or up to the ceiling?" The child may well answer, "Up to the sky!" The child will give you far less information if you just ask if he is happy or angry about the new brother's arrival.

In addition, it is important to remember that a child under seven or eight years of age must be encouraged to *express his feelings physically*, in order to believe it's okay for him to *have* those feelings. He can show you his current feeling about the new addition to the family by pinching, poking, or jumping on the Blob or the Wild Moment Pillow. You can hold the new baby up to watch this show, telling the baby, for example: "Look how big and strong your brother is, and how well he can show me how unhappy he is right now about you joining the family!"

Find ways for the older child to help with the little one, and thank the older child frequently for his assistance. Tell others, in his presence, about specific occasions on which the older child was particularly helpful to you.

Get out pictures of the older child, especially ones that show you giving him the same kinds of attention you now give to the new baby.

When the older child is in good spirits and acting in an age-appropriate way, ask him if he'd like to *play baby,* and have you wrap him up and rock him in the rocking chair as you did when *he* was a little baby.

Give the older child a present from the new baby when the baby first arrives, and keep a few small gifts on hand, also *from the baby,* that can be given to the older child when visitors bring gifts for the new family member.

It is important to have regularly scheduled Special Time with the older child. Be sure to UN-invite the new baby to this activity.

Seven or eight weeks before the new baby is due to arrive, make a book that describes in words and pictures who will be taking care of the older child during the birth and in the days following the birth. The child is concerned with who will get him breakfast, take him to day care, bring him home after day care, and play with him.

There are books on the market on the subject, but a book about the older child's particular situation provides most comfort. The book need not be fancy. Write on pieces of computer paper, and draw pictures (or paste cut-out pictures) to accompany the words. Slip each page into a plastic sleeve, and seal the end of the sleeve with clear tape. Staple the pages together, and read the book to the child every day.

Reinforce the older child's space, belongings, and activities. Frequently point out that baby will not be allowed to play with the older child's toys, play on the swings at the park, or sit with the parent and have stories read to him. When you are going to spend time just with the older child, be sure to tell the new baby in no uncertain terms, in the presence of the older child, that the baby is too little to be allowed to participate in the event.

Let the older child introduce the new baby to visitors. Give the new baby's feet to the older child to touch and hug. This is a lot safer than letting a young child have access to the baby's body and head.

Frequently express your happiness at having a larger, older, more competent child, along with your happiness at having the new baby. At times, express your annoyance with all of the attention the newest family member requires.

Get a Bad Baby Doll for the older child, that can be fed when the mother is feeding the new baby and wrapped up in a blanket when the mother is holding the new baby, and bathed when the new baby is being bathed. The Bad Baby Doll, unlike the family's new baby, doesn't mind being pinched, poked, hit, or being thrown in the trash at times when the older sibling feels that the new baby is commanding too much of the parent's attention. Because the Bad Baby can take any and all negative attention the older child cares to give it, the Bad Baby Doll becomes a cherished belonging.

Here is a letter written to me by the mother of four-year-old Billy, shortly after the birth of Billy's little brother:

"Dear S, Billy is so proud of his new baby brother. The baby is three-weeks-old, and it has been heaven. Billy nurses and burps his Bad Baby Doll when I am nursing the baby. Billy says he wants to hug the baby real hard, but knows that his little brother really is too fragile, so he hugs Bad Baby Doll instead. Of course I've seen a few karate chops land on Bad Baby Doll, but I've seen none from Billy to his real baby brother. All of Billy's kicking my belly and pre-baby tantrums stopped once we made a book about our family, that made the point that the baby would be *added* to the family, and would not *replace* Billy. Let me pass one thing along to you that really worked nicely. We found some blue lollypops that said 'It's a boy.' Billy passed these out both at school and in the neighborhood. He really seemed to enjoy doing that. He even, on his own, told the pharmacist, 'I have a new brother.' But never, *ever, ever* say, when you are pregnant, 'Oh, the baby is kicking!' Or, if you do, quickly say something negative about it. Or you just might get a four-year-old trying to please you by trying to kick you in the belly, to demonstrate how much better he can do it than the baby can!"

# Overview of Child Development
## Chapter 2

### Non-Verbal Language

As discussed in the introduction to this writing, three factors contribute to the naturally occurring and ongoing difficulties in parents communicating with their young children: the young child's inability to recognize what is real and what isn't; the child's lack of reliable verbal language for thinking and self-expression; and the child's inability to use abstract thinking. Before embarking on a trek through the major stages of child development, more needs to be said about the important influence of nonverbal behavior/language.

Movement is a condition of living things. As long as the individual is breathing, he is moving. All nonverbal actions tell us something about his genetic, neurological, physical and emotional developmental history, cultural influence, and current situation.

The importance of the nonverbal interaction that occurs between the infant or young child and her caregivers should not be overlooked. Consider the work of Harlow and his monkeys. In his series of experiments with monkeys, Harlow demonstrated that a baby monkey could develop into a normal adult monkey if provided with a swinging, terrycloth-covered plastic bottle capable of dispensing warm milk. However, if the plastic bottle was stationary, or was not covered in soft terrycloth, or didn't dispense warm milk, the baby monkey's social development was severely impeded. and as an adult, the monkey's social interaction was negatively impacted

Human movement has two aspects that occur simultaneously: functional (*what* action is being taken) and qualitative (*how* the person takes the action).

Far from being a far out theoretical construct, the notation system developed by Rudolph Laban makes possible exact notation and replication of both aspects of any movement or movement sequence. Use of this notation system allows a trained observer to accurately record the functional and qualitative aspects of an entire dance performance in France and send it to Argentina, where the ballet can be exactly replicated in performance. Researchers like Marian North and Martha Davis have validated the proposition that the movement repertoire (the frequency of quantitative and qualitative aspects of an individual's movements) will repeat every forty-five minutes as long as the individual is awake.

This method of observation and notation of the two aspects of movement can be used in conjunction with any theoretical framework to establish an accurate description of important aspects of an individual's physical, intellectual, and emotional situation. Our interest here is in its use to describe the course of development of the infant and young child.

At birth, the infant's movement is largely determined by inborn reflexes. Optional movements are only gradually acquired. Part of the infant's genetic givens are movement propensities that begin to appear in the early months of life. The individual's movement repertoire, i.e. the sum total of the quantity and quality of the movements she can make can accurately be described as the visual aspect of the individual's personality. The individual's movement repertoire retains consistency after the first few years of life.

Nonverbal behavior is the first and only reliable language of the infant and young child. Initially it is the *only* way the child can express herself, communicate with others, and make sense out of what she observes and experiences. Because verbal language only develops gradually and isn't reliable until the child is five years old, nonverbal communication continues throughout life to be the carrier of the true emotional meaning of what is verbalized, not just during the first years of life, but throughout life. Effective communication between child and parent is greatly eased after reliable verbal language is available to the child, allowing both child and parent to think and consciously attribute meaning to events in words.

Imagine two mothers, each with a six-month-old infant. The mothers sit on the floor; each has an infant in her lap. Each mother is suddenly bitten on the arm by her teething infant. Both mothers react with shock. One parent yelps, snatches her arm away, cries out in an angry tone, "Don't bite me again!" as she summarily puts the baby down on the floor in front of her. The other parent gasps quietly, withdraws her arm, and says in a gentle voice, "People aren't for biting, here is something that you *can* bite," while she continues to hold the baby and presses a teething toy into his hand.

Neither baby can understand the words spoken by the parent. However, each baby uses nonverbal skills to understand the meaning of this interaction, by associating the quantity and quality of the parent's words with the quantity and quality of the mother's actions.

During the first several years of life, the infant and young child rapidly become expert in nonverbal comprehension and communication. And, although the four-year-old is well on his way to using verbal language to process information and to express himself, his nonverbal thinking and knowledge are evident in his speech.

A four-year-old knows that the dinosaurs he encounters in books are huge, just as his parents are huge (compared to the child), and that they are powerful beings that, when angry, have scary faces and show their teeth. Since dinosaurs and parents are similar in these respects, they must, according to the child's nonverbal thinking, share other characteristics. Therefore, if you ask a four-year-old, in a conversational tone, "Which dinosaurs are in your family?" he will promptly identify which parent is the Tyrannosaurus Rex. The face of an adult asked the same question will register confusion.

There is general agreement among theorists of child development that core elements of an individual's personality are formed during the first five or six years of life, although refinement and modifications do occur after these earliest years of life. Personality is understood as the individual's unique style of coping with internal, continually changing needs while balancing those needs along with the evolving needs and requirements of the external world.

The following pages describe three different ways of looking at these first six years of child development. We will consider Piaget's work on cognitive development—along with Psychoanalytical Theory—along with using energy to think, sense, and make action decisions, as metaphorically illustrated in *The Wizard of Oz*. These three perspectives overlap.

## Piaget and Cognitive Development

Jean Piaget is generally credited with conducting the most detailed, experimentally based investigation of the stages of cognitive development during the early years of life. For example, imagine a little girl of three years of age. The child observes the same amount of liquid being poured into two glass containers, one of which is tall and narrow while the other is short and wide. Asked which container contains more liquid, she will choose the tall and narrow one. To the child, *taller* looks like *more*. Her answer will not change until she acquires what Piaget referred to as conservation of volume.

According to Piaget, humans have an inborn interest in repeating what is known and familiar, as well as an inborn, continuing drive to pursue and invest emotionally and intellectually in what is new. For example, the child enjoys both hearing a favorite story over and over and playing extensively with her favorite toy, while she also enjoys hearing new stories, and playing with new toys. It is necessary to discard current perceptions and beliefs in order to acquire new knowledge or a different perspective on a particular matter. For example, after being nipped by a dog, the young child's previous opinion that dogs are fun to play with may well be rejected in favor of the new belief that some, if not all dogs are dangerous.

## Freud, Erikson, and Psychoanalytic Theory

Freud's original Psychoanalytic Theory focused on emotionally-linked mental activity of an individual during the first five or six years of life, and the lasting emotional significance such activity has on formation of the individual's personality. Freud hypothesized that there are two parts of the mind—conscious and unconscious. Freud considered influence of the latter to be much greater than the former throughout life.

According to Freud, humans are born with two types of psychic, or mental energy that compels the mind to action. These two types of energy are creative (positive) and destructive (negative). He envisioned the existence of three psychic structures in the mind that develop in order to manage the outpourings of the two types of energy. Freud referred to these structures as the Id, Ego, and Superego. These psychic structures begin to develop in a known sequence during the first six years of life. In healthy development the Ego/Adult is increasingly in charge of the individual's action decisions.

| Actions Based On | Psychic Structure |
|---|---|
| What I feel like doing (creating/destroying) | Id / Child |
| What's realistically possible given situation and people involved | Ego / Adult |
| Internalized sense of what is morally right or wrong | Superego / Adult—Parent |

The Id/Child demands the immediate gratification of pouring out both his creative and his destructive energy. For example, sixteen-month-old Bill, wishing to experience the pleasure of playing with the toy with which his sister is playing, unleashes his destructive energy and bites his sister on the arm, causing her to drop the toy. Bill begins to happily play with it, entirely unmoved by his sister's wailing protest.

The Ego/Adult on the other hand, manages intense creative and destructive impulses and desires in the mind, rather than giving in to a compulsion for immediate action. He or she moderates expression of creative and destructive impulses in the light of realistic appraisal of the situation and possible consequences.

For example, Bill, at five years of age, desperately wants to take apart the model train track layout his brother has put together and create a new one. However, he is able to keep his desire to immediately experience this pleasure in check. Development of the Ego allows Bill to consider that anything short of negotiating a mutually satisfying deal with his brother will result in Bill's parents imposing an unpleasant consequence on Bill. Consequently, Bill successfully negotiates a trade with his brother in which his brother gets to play with a toy of Bill's he covets in return for granting Bill permission to rearrange the model train layout.

The Superego/Parent takes moral considerations into account, asking: what should happen here, what is the right thing to do.

By the time Bill is ten years of age, his Superego/Parent is well developed. Wishing to use his brother's bicycle, Bill empathically works out a mutually satisfactory deal with his brother, based on Bill's Super Ego sense of moral correctness, rather than on knowledge of what will befall Bill if he doesn't do this.

According to Freud's Psychoanalytic Theory, the amount of influence the Id, Ego, and Superego exert on the individual changes as they develop during three stages that span the first five years of life. According to Freud, during each of the three stages he envisioned, psychic energy is specifically connected to a particular area of the body, as evinced by the names he gave these stages—the Oral, Anal, and Phallic/Genital.

Psychoanalytic theorist Erik Erikson took Freud's theory of three stages further, positing the powerful influence of important relationships between the child and significant others, along with genetic and environmental factors during the first five years of life. Erikson referred to the three stages of human development and personality formation that occur during these important years as Basic Trust versus Mistrust, Autonomy versus Shame and Doubt, and Initiative versus Guilt.

Psychoanalytic Theory's first Three Stages of Child Development, as seen differently by Freud and Erikson:

| Ages | Freud | Erikson |
| --- | --- | --- |
| 0-18 months | Oral | Basic Trust vs. Mistrust |
| 18-36 months | Anal | Autonomy vs. Shame and Doubt |
| 3-5 years | Genital | Creativity vs. Guilt |

Descriptions of the hallmarks of each of the three stages envisioned by Erikson:

Basic Trust: If all goes well enough during the first eighteen months of life, the individual acquires a core trust in his or her own physical, emotional, and mental abilities and the belief that he or she will receive sufficient help, when necessary, from others in his or her environment.

Autonomy versus Shame and Doubt: When allowed sufficient opportunity to assert the full range of expression of her emotions, within reasonably set limits, the individual learns to realistically assess and emotionally accept the amount of power and responsibility she has in different situations. For example, a two-year-old can assert her own power when she is allowed to choose which toy to take to the playground. She accepts that she may fully express her rage when prevented from climbing onto the table, but not in the room where her parents are having a conversation. And she accepts that her mother decides when it is time to leave for day care.

Creativity versus Guilt: If all goes well enough during this stage, the individual's drive to assert her power *over others*, and independence *from others* shifts to engaging empathically with others and being interested and enjoying a wide variety of activities on her own.

According to psychoanalytically based and cognitive and linguistic theories of child development, there is a vast difference in the way that a young child and an adult think and experience events. Most famously expressed by Freud, but embraced by many other theorists of human development, the idea that the mind possesses both a conscious and a less than conscious component has become widely accepted. According to these views, somewhere between five and six years of age, conscious memory of how one has ascribed meaning to verbal language and prior events is banished to a less than conscious part of the mind, although it continues to exert an influence on important decisions throughout life.

This is the reason, according to such theories, that adults often fail to realize how significantly their childhoods have impacted their adult lives. An adult lacks conscious memory that she once thought that fire engines bring fire. She dismisses the idea that, as a child, she believed the entire person she was as unacceptable because one of her actions was found to be unacceptable. She, in fact, continues to rely on long forgotten child patterns of thought. It is only with great effort (and, most often, professional psychological assistance) that *child thinking* can be brought to conscious awareness and addressed.

As very young children, most of us envisioned doing at least some things differently when we grew up and had families and children of our own. As cognitive skills like perspective and abstract thinking developed, these *corrections* were banished from conscious awareness. Nevertheless they remained powerfully influential.

Thus, adults embark on the adventure of being parents with high hopes. They have a strong belief that, with *conscious* effort, it will be possible to create more satisfactory relationships between their new family members than were experienced in their respective families of origin.

Recognition of the earliest, child-thinking *corrections* would greatly increase the chances of satisfying relationships in the new family. But in the absence of this awareness, the reality is that the new family relationships are likely to reproduce some of the unfortunate patterns in the respective family of origin of each parent-to-be.

What has been presented in this section up to this point is theory. Here is an example of how this might unfold in an individual's life.

Let's follow Mark into his adulthood. He experienced an unhappy, lonely childhood. During the first eighteen years of his life, Mark lived with his parents. Both of his parents worked long hours outside the home, and rarely spent time together as a couple, with Mark, or as a family. Mark was left with caretakers who were *responsible* but who, like his parents, were not emotionally *responsive* to him.

Mark's great interest in all sports was not affirmed by his parents. To his sadness, they did not help him get involved with sports activities outside of school, and rarely attended the school sports events in which Mark enthusiastically participated. Along with genetic givens, Mark's core perception of who he was as an individual was strongly influenced by the overall tenor of experiences and the meanings he attributed to them during the early years of his life; Mark saw himself as *he who was alone and lonely*.

During the early school grades, Mark formulated a *correction* for his future, when he would be a grown up with his own family, which he believed would lead him to a happier life. Therefore, as an adult, when it came time to seek a life partner, Mark looked for a person who could spend lots of time with him, and with any children they might have. In addition, he vowed that he would support his child's involvement in all sports activities.

He chose an occupation that made only moderate demands on his time, so he would have lots of time to spend with a wife and any children they might have. In fact, he married a woman who wanted to be a stay at home wife and mother. Mark was happy, believing that he had set the stage for a far different life for himself than the one experienced in his childhood.

However, several years and a child later, Mark was very unhappy, and felt as lonely as he ever did as a child. While it is true that his wife was at home, she was busy with numerous projects and activities, and was rarely emotionally available to him or to their son. In addition, their child was less than thrilled to be involved in all kinds of sports activities, and would have happily done without his father's enthusiastic support and involvement in school required sports activities. The child did not enjoy attending sporting events for which his father enthusiastically got tickets. Mark's son had a real interest in music, and would have loved to have had trumpet or drum lessons.

Clearly, Mark made choices that resulted in continuation of his core self-perception that he was and will always be essentially alone and lonely. He duplicated the temporal and emotional distance he had experienced in his original family with his wife and son in his new family. How did this happen, in spite of Mark's conscious efforts to do otherwise?

Corrections envisioned by very young Mark were limited to concrete *child thinking*. He could only envision that making changes in *physical reality* would lead to more happiness for him. Considering desire and capacity for *emotional closeness* between his parents, or between himself and his parents, were abstract concepts unavailable to Mark.

Consequently, the subconscious motivations that he was wholly unaware of drove him to choose a wife who was physically present, without recognizing that she had very limited desire and capacity for emotional presence with him. He provided practical parental involvement in sports activities that his parents had not provided in his own childhood, but couldn't imagine how to provide the emotional closeness he could have enjoyed with his own son if he had embraced his son's interest in musical pursuits.

At this point we return for a last bit of theory. The child doesn't develop the ability to think beyond the limits of physical reality until somewhere between the ages of nine and eleven years of age. The world of abstractions—internal emotional states, for instance, that are not expressed in some physical action the child can perceive—do not exist for the child. If the parent feels angry inside and yells at the child, the child recognizes *anger action*. If the adult *feels* anger but does not express it, the child perceives no physical manifestation of it. To the child, the parent's internal state does not exist.

In addition, he assumes he is a causal agent in all that he experiences. If his parent yells at him in an angry voice, the child *cannot* believe that he, the child, was not, in some way, to some extent, the cause of the parent's anger. In reality, the parent's anger may have little to do with the child or his behavior.

Unfortunately, adults rarely speak to their children about the disparity between verbal and nonverbal expressions, or about their belief that things happen that have nothing to do with the child. In addition, there is often insufficient discussion about abstractions like internal feeling states, and their consequences on human interactions, even once the child is old enough to think in words and to think abstractly about these things. Such discussions would help the young person develop empathy for himself and for others, and move beyond the limited world of physical realities (concrete quantity of events) to deepening appreciation for emotional states (abstractions like the emotional quality of events).

## Thinking, Sensing and Feelings, Making Action Decisions, and *The Wizard of Oz* as a Metaphor

Psychoanalytic theory as described by the original theorists is not much in favor at present. However, embedded in the stages of early child development, as envisioned by those theorists, are universally relevant descriptions of skills a child must acquire in order to survive and thrive in life:

- Think clearly (pay attention to what is relevant and disregard what is not).
- Acknowledge and be comfortable with a full range of feelings, able to take responsibility for both positive and negative actions.
- Make and carry out empathically-based actions, in order to accomplish tasks both on one's own and in cooperation with others, within given time limits and other situational constraints.

Each of these three skill sets is a hallmark of a specific stage of human development from birth to six years—thinking during the first stage, realistic sensing and accepting personal responsibility during the second, and taking timely and empathically based actions during the third.

In fact, in order to effectively accomplish any task, an individual needs to mobilize a certain amount of energy and to tap into the skills acquired in all three stages.

Regardless of one's theoretical orientation, expenditure of physical, mental, and emotional energy is a condition of human life, applied in cycles of exertion and recuperation as each individual navigates his or her unique way through life.

## Thinking

Effective thinking is inextricably connected with paying attention and ascribing meaning to what is experienced. It involves focusing attention somewhere along a continuum between a single focus (one tree) and multiple (the forest). Clear and effective thinking requires the individual to pay attention only to relevant stimuli, disregard irrelevant stimuli and maintain attention long enough for comprehension.

A newborn has no awareness that she is in any way separate from everyone and everything she experiences. She has no need or ability to think of—that is, to intellectually consider—anyone or anything outside herself, since she is the entire universe of all she experiences.

Awareness that she is an entity and surrounded by a boundary that separates her from other people and objects develops gradually and isn't established until the child reaches eighteen months of age. She therefore attributes meaning to experiences only as they relate to her.

Remember the five-month-old baby who is teething. Her gums are painful and biting something helps relieve her discomfort. She perceives the teething ring, her mother's arm, and her own arm as part of herself, although she quickly becomes aware that clamping her gums on her own arm produces pain!

## Feeling/Sensing

Human beings feel, or sense only four types of emotions. They may be experienced singly or in concert with other emotions. Each type of emotion can be sensed along a continuum of intensity:

    Happiness: ----------------------------bliss / mild pleasure

    Sadness: despair ------------------------a little down

    Anger: fury ----------------------------slightly irritated

    Fear: petrified--------------------------uneasy

People frequently identify thoughts they are having as feelings. For example: "I feel that Sam did the wrong thing" is really a statement about the speaker's thinking. Feelings are attached to physical sensations experienced somewhere in the body by the speaker. For example: "I feel so uneasy about what Sam did, that I have a knot in my stomach."

The infant feels either bliss or intense distress. During the second stage (eighteen to thirty-six months), the child initially prefers expressing feeling extremes. "Me loves you!" "No!" "I not like it!" are familiar refrains. By the end of this stage the child has made enormous strides in ability to appropriately express gradations of the four feelings, and to govern their expression in the light of behavioral constraints if they are insisted on by caretakers.

If things go well enough during the fourth and fifth year of life, the child is aware of, and feels comfortable with the full range of each of the four types of feelings, and for a good deal of the time can express and communicate them effectively in ways that are acceptable.

## Making Action Decisions

It is impossible to take all possible options for action at one time. Therefore, taking action is intricately integrated with making decisions. At birth, the infant's actions are primarily controlled by inborn reflexes. In a few short months, however, the infant begins to make decisions before taking action. For example, when offered two rattles, he reaches for the one he prefers to shake.

As the child moves through the first three or four years of life, he moves from making action decisions based only on his own immediate wishes, to basing them on consideration of the three elements of efficient and effective decision making:

1. His own needs and wishes.

2. Empathic consideration of others who might be impacted by his actions.

3. Constraints of the situation (such as location in a crowded elevator versus walking in a field) and time constraints (it's five minutes before the train leaves and we're late versus we have all day to relax at the lake).

True empathy is now possible. For example, four-year-old Paul was not usually interested in drawing, but went straight to get paper and markers as soon as he got home from nursery school. He drew a picture of a large, shaggy dog. When his mother asked him to tell her about the picture he explained that he made the picture so that his classmate, Bob, could look at what his dog Whiskers looked like whenever he wanted to, so that he wouldn't feel so sad. Paul knew that Bob was sad about the death of Whiskers who was hit by a car a few days before.

Examples that situational constraints are being considered occur when the child chooses to use an *indoor* versus an *outdoor* voice, draws within the borders of the paper, and is able to take turns by easily sharing his favorite toy with a visiting child.

## The Wizard of Oz as Metaphor

*The Wonderful Wizard of Oz*, by Frank L. Baum, first published in 1900, provides an interesting picture of the course of early child development. I refer the reader, if not already familiar with the story, to either the book or the movie.

Like a human infant, Dorothy, the child protagonist in the story, is cast by a tornado (a metaphor for birth) into a world with which she is totally unfamiliar. Like a human infant, she is initially dependent on the aid offered by those she encounters. Dorothy wants to get back to her aunt and uncle in Kansas, but believes she lacks the ability to get herself home (a metaphor for taking care of herself).

Each of the three main characters Dorothy meets personifies a developmentally important skill humans need to acquire during the first six years of life. Each character believes he lacks the skill he personifies. Scarecrow grieves that he doesn't have a brain and therefore cannot think. Tin Woodman believes he lacks a heart and therefore cannot feel. Lion believes he lacks courage and therefore cannot take needed actions.

Dorothy and her three companions believe that only the Wizard of Oz (a metaphor for the parent) can provide each of them with the skills they lack, so they set out to find the all-powerful wizard. Along the way, they encounter difficulties that, through their own efforts and the help of some others, they overcome.

Eventually Dorothy and her companions meet the Wizard of Oz and discover that he is just a man, lacking magical power to grant them the skills they seek. They start to despair. However, the Wizard, like a good parent, encourages them by pointing out that Scarecrow has already used his thinking to help his friends, that Tin Woodman has already demonstrated love for his companions, proving that he does indeed have a heart, and that the Lion has already demonstrated courageous action, on behalf of himself and his friends.

With her skills confirmed, Dorothy (metaphorically the universal child) thinks of herself as a person with good capability to take care of herself. She remembers instructions the good witch Glinda gave her. She takes responsibility for her feelings of sadness at not being back in Kansas, by taking effective action to return her to her aunt and uncle. She clicks the heels of her shoes together three times and commands the shoes to carry her home.

# The First Eighteen Months of Life
## Chapter 3

(Note: for this section the mother is assumed to be the primary caretaker of the infant)

## Pregnancy, Birth, and First Month of the Infant's Life

Pregnancy is a parasitic relationship, in which the fetus will leach whatever it needs from the mother's body. How the mother feels about being pregnant (biological clock, career situation, education, whether planned or unintended pregnancy, spacing of children, etc.) has a significant effect on the early relationship between mother and infant, between the parent partners, and on the partner who did not experience pregnancy and the infant's birth. The social, financial, and emotional situation of the couple, and the extent and duration of any fertility issues prior to the pregnancy, can also significantly impact all of these relationships.

Whether the birth experience meets parental expectations and whether or not there is an adequate opportunity for parents and infant to bond during the first few days of the infant's life impact their early relationship. For instance, the day after his healthy son was born, Stephen, far from expressing happiness, announced that the previous night had been the worst night of his life. There had been a sudden crisis during labor and Stephen had been told that there was a chance that his wife wouldn't survive. Stephen was not able to begin to bond with his son until he was sure that his wife was going to recover fully from the birth.

The influence of each parent's respective family of origin can also be impactful—for instance, the presence of differing expectations in each parent's family of origin about how the infant should be raised, as in "Let the baby cry" versus "You can never give a baby too much attention." It is likely that each parent was less than entirely satisfied with the way things unfolded in his or her respective family of origin. It is likely that as children they envisioned doing things differently when they themselves became parents. However, envisioned changes formulated (as Mark's were in a previous section of this writing) when they were children and lacked ability for abstract thinking—and the *corrections* they initiate in their chosen adult family—often do not have the intended beneficial effect.

Whether or not the child meets the parents' expectations (for instance the sex, appearance, health, and personality of the infant) can strongly influence the relationship between the infant and his parents. So can the role the parents imagine the infant will play in the family (to keep the focus off marital difficulties, for instance, or to add to the couple's current happiness).

The fit between the overall amount of energy of parent and infant and their preferred ways of moving can also affect the relationship between the primary care-taking parent and the child. For example, prior to the birth of her daughter, Sue envisioned cuddling with the new baby a good deal of the time as she and the baby lounged about the house during the three months of maternity leave.

Sue loved her daughter and interacted with her a good deal of the day. However, unlike her friends who had also recently had babies, Sue was exhausted from attending to her daughter by ten o'clock in the morning. Sue's overall energy level was moderate and she preferred to move at a relaxed pace and enjoyed frequent periods of reading, watching a TV show, or browsing the internet on her computer. In movement preferences, she resembled a relaxed seal, happily resting on a rock, enjoying the sunshine pouring down on her.

By sharp contrast, her daughter possessed an inborn high level of energy. She clearly preferred almost constant and rapid movement of her limbs, and spent hours focusing on, and trying to capture the mobiles strung above the changing table, crib, and stroller. In movement preferences, she resembled a spider, trying to rapidly complete the spinning of her web.

When this difference in styles of moving through their days was pointed out to Sue, she felt better about the fatigue she was experiencing. She observed for herself that the disparity between the movement preferences of her friends and their respective infants was not nearly as pronounced.

The infant's primary task during the first month is to recover from birth, integrate muscle groups, and regulate vital bodily functions (respiration, circulation, communication, heat regulation, reflexes, digestion, elimination, sensory perception). His survival is dependent on the mother's ability to establish and maintain a mutually dependent, symbiotic relationship with him. This includes a communication system allowing mother and infant to interpret and respond to each other's actions with exquisite accuracy.

Initially, the infant lacks awareness of what is within him, what is external to him, and the location, nature and permeability of the boundary between himself and his mother. If there are two parents, and one is the primary caretaker of the infant, the other parent must be willing to assume a supporting role to the intense relationship between infant and primary caretaker mother.

Parental tolerance is sorely tested by sleep deprivation and unpredictable disruptions in management of household tasks, work, social, and intimate life. Maintenance of a reasonable balance between the needs of the infant, the parents as individuals and as a couple, and the needs of other members of the immediate and extended family during this period of adjustment is unlikely.

## Thinking and Paying Attention

Thinking is only required if there is awareness that there is something outside the self that, along with the self, must be taken into consideration. During the first three months of life the infant perceives that everything he experiences (and therefore all that exists) is part of himself, so there is no need for the child to think. The symbiotic relationship between mother and the totally helpless infant during the first three months of life supports the infant's perception that he and his mother are one entity. On both a physical and emotional level, mother and infant experience a mutual need for contact with one another. The boundary between them is permeable.

When a nursing mother hears her baby cry, or just thinks about him when she is not with him, milk reflexively begins to flow from her breasts. When nursing her infant while sitting in a rocking chair, the rate at which the mother rocks (usually out of conscious awareness) is in mathematical proportion to the rate of the infant's sucking. When the mother is playing with the infant, or walking about holding the infant, mother and infant are in a constant movement conversation with one another.

Most of the time the mother adjusts the quality of her movements to match those of her infant. For example, when the baby is flailing his arms and legs in an agitated way the mother will gently bounce the baby up and down in her arms in time with the flailing to convey to the infant that he (meaning he and his mother merged together) can calm himself.

Occasionally the mother finishes her shower, letting the infant fuss for a bit before she attends to his needs. Both kinds of experiences (clashing and attuning) are essential for development of the infant's awareness—that he is an important being, and that he is separate from other beings and objects—that he is not, in fact, the entire universe.

The infant's tolerance for not receiving immediate parental attention increases dramatically from three to eighteen months of age for two reasons.

First, his repertoire of chosen rather than reflexively controlled activity increases. This allows him to sustain and entertain himself for short periods of time. Second, during the latter part of this stage the child begins to develop what is called object constancy. This is the ability to think that people and objects continue to exist even though they are not immediately available to his senses (sight, hearing, smell, taste, touch).

Evidence that object constancy has begun to appear occurs when the child who is sitting up searches for an object he has recently watched someone place behind his (the child's) back. Prior to this, when not in direct sensory contact with people and objects, he thinks they have ceased to exist.

When such contact is reestablished, the child thinks that the object or person has literally been *re-created*. This is why, when needing or wanting contact with his absent mother, an infant is often inconsolable. He is bereft. His mother has ceased to exist. He has no capacity as yet to think that she will be *re-created*.

When the infant is awake and content, parent and infant can experience conversations with facial expressions and sounds, as well as by moving together. In those conversations the parent's actions alternate between matching and differing from the infant's. The infant begins to imitate behaviors modeled by his parent when they are close to motions he can already make.

When the parent smiles at him, he tries to smile back at the parent, and the parent then smiles again. Appearance of a social smile at about three months of age is a clear sign of awareness that other people and objects are not entirely part of himself. These very real conversations between parent and child encourage the infant to *think* of himself as a responsible and responsive partner in a reciprocal relationship with his parents.

After the first three months, the infant's attention and thinking expand from initial interest in his own body to his parents and objects in physical proximity to him. He begins to pay attention to interesting environmental events and tries to discover the actions that produced them. In this way he is thinking in action.

For instance, suppose a three-month-old suddenly releases the rattle he has been reflexively holding. It disappears from his sight and touch. He will visually search the area it previously occupied in his visual field, vocally signal distress that the rattle has ceased to exist, and search for the rattle physically by continuing the reflexive grabbing motions he used when the rattle was in his hand. If the rattle is replaced in his hand by his parent, the infant experiences pleasure.

Images of such emotionally meaningful action sequences are formed and held in the infant's mind. Acquisition of these mental action plans, or schemas, proceeds at a rapid pace, and soon they are strung together in sequences that are forerunners of the thinking (paying and sustaining attention) which eventually occur in the absence of physical action.

The schemas are combined in an increasingly systematic way and eventually he has one plan (or schema) to reach a goal, and a second to deal with the goal. For instance, he can reach for his bottle, and then tilt it upwards and drink from it. His thinking then begins to drive his purposeful behavior to do things that he hasn't done before. For example, he reaches for the bottle, grabs it, and throws it over the crib railing.

When the child acts on the environment and gets predictable results, schemas and combinations of schemas are formed into generalizations and categorizations that are the forerunners of practical logic that will eventually be internalized and stored in the child's mind.

One can tell experiences are being stored when the child looks for a toy in the most *recent* place he saw it before it disappeared, as opposed to where it was when he *first* saw it disappear. For example, as fourteen-month-old Peter watched, his mother covered a toy truck with a blanket, then removed the truck from under the blanket, showed it to Peter, and then put the truck under a pillow. At this point she asked her son where the toy was. Peter went directly to the pillow, and pulled out the truck.

Forerunners of ability to think of more than one possibility, and to take another person's point of view into consideration, appear during the first eighteen months of life, as the child acquires awareness of something outside herself. Once the infant's attention extends beyond herself, she can focus on a single action or person (for example the bottle from which she is drinking or the toy she is holding).

Next, she can focus on two actions or objects simultaneously—for example, holding her stuffed teddy bear while reaching for a cookie. By the end of this stage she can pay attention and think simultaneously about three things. For example, she holds a block in each hand, while her parent offers her a third block to hold. The child tucks one of the blocks she is holding under her arm and grasps the one being offered to her.

Thinking is also learned on a physical level as the infant experiences repeated pairing of events or objects—for example, mother goes with baby, milk goes with feelings of hunger. The child's ability to discriminate between helpful and unhelpful stimuli, and to choose the former, develops. For instance, the child prefers to chew on a teething biscuit, not a building block.

When my daughter was young I wanted to limit her sugar intake, so I used the word "cookie" for both cookies and crackers. She accepted a cracker in place of a cookie until she was seventeen months old—until the day when I extended a cracker to her and she shook her head and responded, "Want other cookie."

Discriminating between relevant and irrelevant stimuli develops. This is the precursor of ability to pay attention to what the teacher is saying in first grade rather than to be distracted by the airplane the child can see through the classroom window—the same ability that eventually helps a person focus on the main idea versus tangential comments of a lecturer.

The child also acquires the ability to recognize relationships of objects and events. For example, he removes an obstacle in front of the object he wants to retrieve; he anticipates events that don't depend on his own actions (when his siblings come home, the house will be noisy); and he expects people to act in certain ways—for instance, when he falls and cries, he expects that he will be picked up and comforted.

## Language and Music Development

The infant's speech development begins with random production of disorganized, babbling sounds that gradually expand to include the whole range of the infant's voice. Within the first three months, the infant is gradually able to regulate and imitate some sounds and qualities of sounds that he hears and recognize the effectiveness of sounds that he makes. For example, the intensity of the infant's crying begins to subside when he hears his mother's voice responding to his urgent crying.

Real sound conversations are possible during these very early months of the infant's life. The parent starts by imitating a sound accidentally made by the infant and waits to see if that sound is repeated. If it is, the parent makes the same sound again. After going back and forth in that conversation, the parent makes a slight variation in the sound (in pitch, or number of times it's repeated) to see whether the infant will imitate that variation.

The infant's ability to comprehend spoken language develops far sooner, and proceeds at a vastly quicker pace than his ability to produce it. Shana was gathering up the toys her seven-month-old daughter Lauren had tossed behind her as she stood in her playpen. Shana mused to herself, "Now what did I do with that teddy bear?"

Lauren gazed with interest at her mother, sat down, looked around the playpen, picked up the teddy bear, stood up, and silently held it out to her mother. Unsure that her daughter had really understood what had been said, Shana placed the teddy bear behind her daughter in the playpen, and in a few minutes again said, "Now where did I put that teddy bear?"

Her daughter gave her a long look, retrieved the toy, and held it out to her mother. She had clearly understood her mother's words.

Claudia had been speaking some Spanish to her son since her son's birth, but had no idea how much of it had been sinking in. Showing her son, now fourteen months old, a photograph of a dog surrounded by a lot of toys, Claudia asked, "Donde esta el perro?" (Where is the dog?) Her son immediately pointed to the dog.

The child's ability to comprehend and speak sign language is available many, many months before audible language can be produced, and can greatly enhance effective communication between parent and child. There are well-written and illustrated books available on the subject.

Development of the muscles involved in producing spoken speech proceed from the back to the front of the mouth, so ease in producing the sound of letters in the alphabet varies according to difficulty. For instance, the letter "L" requires placement of the tongue at the front of the mouth, behind the front teeth, making it one of the later sounds a child can produce. Therefore, seventeen-month-old David referred to his older sister, Lisa, as either Sa or Weesa.

Parents of very young children tend to use higher pitched, sing-song voices when talking to their young children than they do when speaking to older children and adults. This instinctive interaction actually fosters development of spoken language.

Children acquire comprehension of spoken language by the close conjunction in time of a spoken word and the action that accompanies it. Singing to the child, and exposing him to chants and rhymes which have accompanying motions that both parent and child can make, are very helpful. For example, songs like "Old MacDonald" link the name of an animal with the sound that animal makes. Songs like "The Wheels On the Bus," "Open, Shut Them," and "Where is Thumbkin?" all link words with their attendant motions. The child can imitate parts of the actions that go along with these songs somewhere around nine months of age.

Chanting rhythmically about events that frequently repeat in the child's day is also helpful, especially for parents who are not comfortable singing—for instance, chanting, "Now we go and get our lunch," or "Here we go to the changing table." The child's attention is carried along primarily by the rhythm of the song or chant, and he will sometimes accompany these chants with his own rhythmic motions or sounds.

Singing or chanting should be done at a pace that allows the child to join you with accompanying motions or sounds the child has the physical capacity to make himself. Unfortunately, an overwhelming amount of commercially produced music for children is available on every conceivable electronic device. Almost all of it is played far, far too fast for even the *possibility* of the child to sing along with it, let alone follow any accompanying motions. Muscles in his mouth and body simply cannot move that quickly.

The more the child is exposed to singing and spoken language, the better for speech development. Parents should read to the child as soon as the child can attend to the illustrations in a book. Vary the tones of your voice when you read and point to the illustrations, asking the child to identify the part of the illustration that has to do with the written text you are reading.

Parents can expose the child to additional meaningful spoken language by telling the child about emotionally significant events in the parents' own daily lives. This is best done using the same varied tones of voice you would use if trying to keep an adult friend interested in the events you are recounting. Remember how difficult it is to listen to a lecture given by someone who speaks in a monotone. Variety in voice tone, pitch, and excitement can make even eating vegetables sound like an adventure!

## Sensing and Feelings: Assessing Responsibility

Initially the infant only feels a pervasive sensation of bliss (happiness), or disaster (a combination of sadness, anger, and fear). There is no middle range of feelings. When experiencing disaster, the infant can signal his upset by movement and/or sound, but he is dependent on the parent to respond to his signals in ways that help him return to a state of bliss. At times, some variation of the following sequence is effective in helping the infant return to this state:

The mother picks the infant up and holds him so that their two bodies fit together as comfortably as possible. If the infant's upset continues, Mom moves in such a way that the rhythm, intensity, and speed of her motions matches those of the infant she is holding. For example, the mother starts by moving her arms from side to side and up and down, in time with the infant's cries and waving limbs. As the infant calms, the mother's motions become less and less energetic, but they still follow the rhythm of the infant's motions. When the infant is close to being restored to a state of bliss, the mother uses gentle rocking motions in time with the infant's breathing rate. Singing or humming a song with a strong rhythm may encourage the infant's body to calm.

At times, however, this sequence does not work. It should be remembered that the infant's language is nonverbal behavior. Because of her intense and intimate relationship with the infant, the mother often becomes very upset at the infant's upset. The infant reads his mother's upset loud and clear via physical contact with her body, and this magnifies and intensifies the infant's own upset.

Mothers often find this fact difficult to believe. They believe it possible to conceal their own upset through conscious effort. They believe they will be able to hold the infant in a way the infant will perceive as relaxed and comforting. It is far easier to outwit a Lie Detector!

Fortunately there are other effective techniques to use in order to soothe an upset infant. What they all have in common is separating the infant from the mother's body when she is herself upset. Some infants are calmed by being placed in an infant seat that is then placed on top of a dryer or washing machine that is running. Or the infant can be secured in an infant seat, which is then placed in the middle of a large hammock, at a ninety-degree angle from the anchored ends of the hammock. The period of the swing can be varied and adjusted to match the emotional state of the infant.

Another option is to place the infant on his back in the middle of a waffle weave blanket. The four corners of the blanket are firmly grasped, and the infant is swung back and forth, in rhythm with the infant's breathing. The weave of the blanket allows the infant to experience something like the gentle sloshing experienced in utero, which conveys to the infant that his mother is with him.

There are a number of infant swings and seats with mechanical rocking mechanisms, some with variable speed. While these may help, their effectiveness is limited by the fact that their speed cannot be attuned to the rhythms of the infant.

What the infant experiences during the first eighteen months of life provides the foundation for development of what Erikson refers to as "Basic Trust or Mistrust" in himself and in the world. What the infant experiences during this period also lays the foundation for eventual development of true empathy, which involves recognizing one's separateness from others.

Ability to experience and express gradations and combinations of feelings increases substantially during the first eighteen months of life. With respect to sensing personal responsibility, he feels good about the happiness he experiences and attributes it entirely to his own actions. However, he holds other people and objects entirely responsible for any and all negative feelings he experiences.

If a sixteen-month-old bumps his head on the doorway, and begins to cry, the parent can usually help by slapping the doorway and saying, "Bad doorway, to bump my baby's head." When the pain from the bump subsides, the child will probably enjoy smacking the doorway in like fashion.

## Making Decisions and Taking Action

For the first two or three months of life, almost all of the infant's activity is controlled by reflexes, so no real decision making occurs. The inborn reflexes are:

- Blinking: infant reacts to a puff of air or light in the eyes.
- Babinski: when the bottom of the foot is touched the toes spread and the foot is flexed.
- Moro: sudden loss of support causes limbs to flap and then be drawn in towards the body.
- Rooting: when placed in a nursing position or when cheek is touched, the infant's mouth opens, sucking motions start, and his head turns towards the side that was touched as his mouth searches for a nipple.
- Stepping: when infant is held upright and one foot touches the ground, the other foot is flexed, so feet move in a walking pattern.
- Sucking: infant will suck on whatever object placed in his mouth.
- Grasping: the infant will clutch an object placed in the palm of his hand. A newborn can cling with his fingers and hands so strongly that he can support his entire body.
- Swimming: when placed in water, infant makes coordinated swimming motions.
- Tonic Neck Response: when the head is moved to the left, the left limbs straighten and the right limbs flex. When the head is moved to the right, the right limbs straighten and left limbs flex.
- Swallow: allows the infant to take in nourishment.
- Head lifting: when placed on his tummy the infant will lift his head.
- Startle: the way the infant moves when startled remains fairly constant throughout his life. Most often the eyes widen, and limbs move away from the trunk.

In his book, *The Happiest Baby On The Block,* Dr. Harvey Karp describes how to turn off what he believes to be a crying reflex. He outlines a number of effective infant soothing methods, including placing the infant in close proximity to a vacuum cleaner that has been turned on! These methods are demonstrated with a variety of infants in Dr. Karp's videotape of the same name. I strongly recommend this book and its accompanying videotape.

During the first two months when awake, the infant's entire body is in constant, generalized motion. There is no purposive coordination of movement between his body parts. His limbs move independently of one another and alternate between moving away from his trunk and moving inward, towards it. His head moves from side to side.

The infant's movements occur in three types of rhythms, which occur in different combinations of body parts at different times. These rhythms are: sucking (think of the way a kitten's paws move when it is nursing), biting (think of the way a baby rapidly moves his hands up and down when frustrated), and chewing (think of a baby grabbing onto and holding an object that he waves around).

During these first months, muscle groups become integrated so that emotional and physical needs (respiration, digestion, need for warmth, attention, and stimulation) are regulated and can be expressed and communicated. At this point real choice begins to emerge in the infant's actions. The infant not only focuses intently on faces and objects in his visual field, he begins to move his head to follow an object being moved slowly across his visual field. He chooses to smile at faces he recognizes.

His hands make grabbing motions while he watches a moving mobile. After repeated accidental batting of an object suspended above him but within his reach, he can eventually grasp and hold onto the object.

Control over cycles of holding his energy back (for example, gazing at a toy for a time instead of trying to grab it at first sight) and releasing his energy in chosen actions increases. His ability to use gradations of energy allows him to signal his discomfort, and then wait to see if the parent responds, rather than immediately experiencing and broadcasting emotional disaster.

Control over his chosen actions develops from whole body to gestural (movements of arms and hands, legs and feet), and from gross to fine motor coordination (from swiping all the toasted oats cereal off the high chair tray to being able to pick them up one at a time), and from head to toes (hands can grasp each other long before the infant can lift his two legs in concert).

From four to six months, the infant's body gradually assumes a rectangular shape, and his movements become increasingly chosen, purposeful, and controlled. He develops ability to roll from tummy to back, and then from back to tummy.

By six months of age, his arms and legs move in concert with each other. He enjoys grabbing onto his toes with his two hands. He can hold his head erect when in a sitting position and may be able to sit up and move from side to side.

He grabs and explores objects using both hands in a coordinated fashion. Exploration of objects usually includes placing them in his mouth, a destination of particular interest to him. Whatever the child does that is pleasing to him, he does over and over and over. He is interested in both new and familiar objects and shows particular interest in a few favorite toys.

In the latter part of his first year, the child begins to try to propel himself forward on his tummy, often using swimming motions of his arms and legs. This gradually evolves into some form of crawling. His innate interest in what is new results in an extreme interest in this newest activity. At this point the parents usually attempt to baby-proof their living space.

At nine months, with the now well-developed pincer grasp typical of this stage, Alice picked up whatever tiny objects she found on the floor, and placed them in her mouth for further investigation. For a time, whenever her mother approached her, Alice automatically opened her mouth so that her mother could remove whatever object had recently taken up residence there.

The child encounters large objects that impede her forward progress as she crawls along. She also encounters the nylon mesh borders of her crib or playpen. This leads to attempts to stand. When standing is mastered, she becomes very interested in cruising about on her feet while holding onto a stable object or a parent's hands. When sitting, she can reach behind herself to retrieve an object that she knows has been placed there.

The infant's overall body shape continues to widen until, at a year old, the child resembles a cylinder on two legs that move up and down like pistons in a car engine. Her body doesn't convey that she's going in a particular direction as much as it conveys "Here I am, upright." She enjoys playing patty cake and peekaboo, imitates sounds, recognizes her own name, waves bye bye, crawls, stands, and may walk on her own. As she moves, she has no sense of caution, so the parent must be vigilant about ensuring the child's safety.

Because experiencing pain is unpleasant to the child, she would like to see pain as an external object rather than as part of herself, so she attributes pain to her parent. She may then choose to hit the parent, because in the eyes of the child, the parent is the hurt itself.

By this age, it is possible to observe the child's inborn preference for how far from her body she chooses to move her limbs (keeping them close to her body, at mid arm's length, or fully extended arm's length). It is also possible to observe the individual's preference for visual, auditory, or kinesthetic involvement with her environment.

For example, Clara attended a weekly discussion group for mothers and their infants. The mothers sat in chairs placed in a circle. Infants were placed in infant seats on the floor in front of their respective mothers. The sessions were videotaped.

Clara was concerned that her five-month-old son, Michael, wasn't as active as the other infants in the group. The group's leader invited Clara to review the videotape of a recent session. It was true that Michael moved around less than most of the other infants. However, viewing the tape demonstrated that Michael had a strong preference for visual activity. He focused on one of the other infants, then scanned the circle of parents, visually located that infant's parent, stared at that parent, and then looked back at that parent's infant. Then Michael moved his gaze to another infant and repeated the exercise of matching infant and parent. This visual activity continued until Michael had matched all of the infants with their respective parents. Watching the taped session allowed the group leader to reassure that Michael was, in his preferred way (visually) as active as the other infants.

Some years later, when observed in his second grade classroom, Michael's preference for visually checking out new situations before engaging more fully in physical activity remained evident.

Once the infant can choose the actions he takes, he chooses actions he thinks will result in pleasure. If he experiences displeasure, he protests and tries to flee or to destroy the source of his displeasure. His action decisions are entirely egocentric.

He achieves an increasing ability to organize and effectively execute his action decisions. For example, he will crawl towards his mother when he wishes to be held or nursed. However, when he refrains from biting the mother's breast, or from touching a forbidden object, he is doing so because he will experience displeasure as a result of the parent's reaction to his action, not because he knows it is the *right* thing to do. In the same way, he will choose not to bite the nipple on a bottle only because that results in stopping the flow of milk.

At about fifteen months of age the child's actions indicate increasing awareness that he is, to some extent, a being separate from his mother. The child toddles away from his mother to explore something of interest to him.

He engages with the object for a time, and then toddles back to his mother, arms open, clearly wanting to be received by her with a hug. However, as soon as he is received into his mother's arms, he turns and quickly toddles away from her again, to explore something else. This repeats over and over.

The child's actions are fueled by increasing awareness of the presence in himself of emerging ambivalent feelings about being an independent being. When his mother does things for him he fears this means loss of his own self. However, wanting to do things for himself fuels his fear that he will lose his mother because he won't need her. This ambivalence increases as he enters the next stage of development.

# Activities

## Activities for the First Months of Life

The infant has an inborn interest in the human face, so place your face close to the infant's face and try, with words and sounds, to interest the child in looking at your face. Play times with the infant should be frequent and last as long as the infant sustains interest in it. Parents should respond to the child's initiated facial expressions, sounds, and actions.

Gently and rhythmically move the infant's arms together and then his legs together in time with rhymes like "Pat-a-Cake." Try to have sound imitation conversations with the infant.

The infant needs a variety of interesting objects on which to visually focus. Hang mobiles above the changing table, playpen, and crib. Look for mobiles that have the dangling objects most highly visible from the infant's vantage point rather than the adult's. Mobiles encourage visual focusing along with coordinated eye-hand reaching and grabbing behavior. Mobiles make diaper changes more interesting for the infant, and therefore easier for the parent.

A variety of objects need to be placed where the infant's hands and feet will touch them, initially accidentally (reflexively), later by choice. Suspend soft toys from a carriage or side of a crib in such a way as to permit the infant to bat at and possibly grab the toy.

Try out different baby carriers to see which best suits the infant—the infant often has a clear preference for one over all others. Some infants prefer to face their mother when in the carrier; some prefer to be able to look outward.

Place brightly-colored socks on the infant's feet, and move his feet in and out of his visual field. Continue to do it when he can raise his legs up together. When he can grab his toes, he may enjoy trying to pull the socks off.

## Activities for the Middle Months
### (sitting up to standing up)

In a child-proofed room with his mother, the child should be allowed to explore spaces and objects on his or her own. Help should only be offered when the child clearly asks for it.

Six-month-old Lisa's mother got a lesson in the importance of that. Lisa was sitting on the floor in her great grandmother's kitchen. Lisa began reaching for a toy that was nearby, but out of her reach. Lisa looked up expectantly at her mother, who started to get the toy for Lisa. Lisa's great grandmother quickly and quietly extended her arm to block the mother's action, saying quietly, "Let's see what she does."

Lisa rocked back and forward for a bit, finally lurched forward onto her stomach, and *swam* to the toy which she then grabbed. Lisa smiled at the toy and, of course, put the toy into her mouth.

Rotate the toys available to the child every few days. Storing one kind of toy in a single small carton or other small container makes the toys more interesting than if different kinds of toys are all jumbled together in one large container.

The child is extremely interested in the directions of "in and out." Letting the child repeatedly empty the cabinet where pots and pans, plastic containers, and other safe-to-play-with objects are stored is an unending source of entertainment for the child.

Covering and uncovering objects is also of continuing interest to the child. Cover a toy with a cloth, and then ask the child where the object is. Toys that attach to each other with self sticking-strips, like pieces of wooden pretend food, are also of interest and help to advance hand strength.

## Activities for Twelve to Eighteen Months of Life

Try to engage the child in the motions that accompany songs like "Eensy Teensy Spider," "Here We Go Round the Mulberry Bush," "The Wheels On the Bus," "I'm a Little Teapot," and "It's Raining, It's Pouring."

Let the child explore playgrounds, and playground equipment, and run in safe open spaces like shopping malls.

If the child is not in daycare, or doesn't spend regular time with a few other children, arrange get-togethers with one or two other children about the same age, once or twice a week. Constant adult supervision will be needed at this age.

Sets of building blocks of different sizes, stuffed animals and dolls, and vehicles of all descriptions are all of great interest to the child.

## Family Life

During the second half of the first year of the infant's life, the mother needs to pull back from the intense emotional and physical involvement with the child on which the infant's survival initially depended. This is necessary for the infant's development as a separate and independently capable being. It can be difficult for the mother to do this. As demanding as the relationship with her infant has been up to this point, this moving apart may well be experienced by the mother as a huge loss.

It is also in the best interest of the family as a whole if the parents pull together again as a couple, nurturing their relationship, *not talking about the baby*. The other parent may encounter resistance on the part of the mother, but should persevere. A single parent needs to have regular, meaningful contact with other adults who are emotionally significant in his or her life.

Even if time is extremely limited (by work schedule or needs of other family members), parents need to ensure that there is provision for regularly-occurring time for older children to spend time with each parent, for the parents to spend time with each other as a couple, and for family, as a whole, to enjoy time together. It is also very important to remember that setting aside time for each parent to pursue his or her own interests is restorative, and that such self-care is not selfish.

## Self-Image – If All Goes Well Enough

If things go well enough, the child's internal bodily systems (respiration, digestion, etc.) are working well. The child believes she has sufficient ability to express and communicate her needs and wishes to the significant others in her life, and that these others will respond in nurturing ways. A two-way, mutually reliable, and responsible system of communication between child and primary caretakers has been established and enjoyed.

The child doesn't clearly distinguish between what she experiences physically and what she experiences emotionally, but all of her experiences have become a lasting part of her developing personality, including Basic Trust in her own abilities and in the world that she experiences.

The child has increasing respect for the boundary between herself and others with whom she shares physical, emotional, and intellectual time and space. Because she no longer thinks she is the universe and can experience more than just two states of beings (satisfactory and unsatisfactory), she thinks and pays attention to what goes on outside of herself, as well as to signals from her own body. For example, she makes a sound that signals her need for attention, and she can wait a bit to see if her parent responds to it, before ratcheting up her signals and announcing disaster.

She treats herself and objects the way that she herself has been treated. Her favorite activity involves repeatedly putting objects into other things and then taking them out. She especially enjoys testing out the properties of objects by putting them in her mouth. She is interested in doing this with both favorite toys and new toys. She is very interested in other children.

Her spoken vocabulary is growing very fast, but not nearly as fast as her ability to comprehend words that she hears. She likes being read to, and can often point to the correct objects in her favorite books when her parent asks her to identify them.

What is real is what she experiences with her senses in the moment. What she cannot sense, or what has been absent for a time that exceeds her tolerance for its absence, does not exist. When her parents are absent for too long, she gets upset because she has no way of knowing that her parents will be *re-created*. Keeping her special blanket or toy with her for the duration may allow her some sense of continuing connection with her parent.

She has preferences for taking in information visually, aurally, or kinesthetically. She also has preferences for moving her limbs in near, mid, or far distance from her body. She can crawl and walk on her own and enjoys exploring new surroundings, especially when her parent is with her.

## Difficulties Linked to This Stage That May Emerge Later

The individual may have difficulty recognizing and honoring the boundary between himself and others: He interrupts what another is saying, stands too close for the other person's comfort, always commands center stage in social situations, or may have difficulty protecting himself from spatial invasions by others.

He may have difficulty feeling complete as a person and therefore feels the need for the addition of a substance or activity to an addictive extent. He may need constant attention from those around him; have difficulty accepting minor criticism; and/or balancing his own needs and desires with the needs of others in a realistic way. He has difficulty trusting the efficacy of his own efforts and those of others, and difficulty maintaining a generally positive outlook on life's possibilities.

# Eighteen to Thirty-Six Months of Life
# Chapter 4

## Use of Energy

The primary use of the child's energy during this stage is for exploration of the full range of his feelings (happy, sad, angry, scared). He uses his energy to conduct almost constant experiments to determine when and where he has the power to announce his feelings and when and where their expression in action will be tolerated.

## Thinking and Paying Attention

Thinking is inextricably linked to paying attention. In order to accomplish any task, and to make meaningful sense of what is being experienced, some stimuli are disregarded, others chosen. Thinking and paying attention needs to be directed at chosen stimuli for sufficient time (brief or sustained) to allow adequate comprehension.

During this stage, the child moves from only thinking and attributing meaning to events via nonverbal actions, to doing so in words. If the child has chosen an activity for his focused attention, his attention span is every bit as long an adult's. The difficulty is getting the child to pay attention to a subject or task chosen *for* the child by another.

The child still lacks the ability for abstract thinking and cannot understand that he is not causally involved in all that he experiences.

Leveling consequences on the child that emphasize the parents' power over the child interferes with development of the child's ability to realistically assess the power he possesses in situations relative to that possessed by others in that situation. So does failing to impose reasonable consequences on the child.

It is important to remember that the child's understanding of justice is the Talion Law (an eye for an eye, you hit me, so I will hit you). He assumes his parents think as he does, including feeling as intensely positive and negative towards him as he does towards them. Therefore he believes his parents wish to visit justice on him in just the ways he wishes to visit it upon them.

However, he is aware that he is much smaller and possesses far less power than they do. Consequently, he fears the magnitude of the consequences which his parents may impose on him. Care needs to be taken to choose a consequence which matches realistic (not Talion) assessment of the child's unacceptable behavior.

The parent is more likely to have the child's full attention in an activity if the child can be helped to see the connection between the activity and a real situation he wants or needs to master. For instance, "Playing by yourself while I wash the dishes means that we can stay longer at the playground."

The child will also be encouraged to pay attention when the parent tells the child what displeased the parent about his behavior—and what he can do to change the situation and therefore your reaction to it. For example, "You are standing too close to me. If you stand at least one arm's length from me, I'll feel more like listening to you."

The parent will be more effective at keeping the child's attention by lowering him or herself to the child's eye level, instead of looming over him.

Understanding abstract concepts like, "taking a stand," "having one's feet on the ground," "getting knocked off my feet," "refusing to let something weigh me down," "lighten up," "that's beside the point," will be learned primarily through pairing the child's physical experiences and the associated verbal language to which he is exposed.

He doesn't distinguish between mental, physical, and social reality. If it moves, it's alive. If aware of its physical existence (a parent or object such as a toy or the moon), he thinks it may be as alive as the child knows himself to be.

His concept of moral law is egocentric: "If I want, and am physically able to do something, then it is the right thing to do. Since I am what I do, if you prevent me from doing the right thing (what I want to do) or consequence me for doing it, you are negating the person that I am. That makes you wrong and bad."

He lacks the mental operations to understand the concepts of number/how many (one, two, some too many), cause and effect (I wanted it, so I should be able to take it), and the non-reversibility of time (Nanna died so she won't visit today. She will visit next Saturday.). The child is working on a more reality-based understanding and acceptance that merging with his parent is not possible, and that he cannot remain a baby forever. The line between fantasy and reality is not yet firmly set. However, he works on sorting out what is real and what is not. He needs opportunities to assert his personal power and to experience restrictions on such assertions. This helps the child to become willing to give up his fantasy that he is and should be accepted as an all-powerful being.

Halloween costumes may be terrifying to a two-year-old who is not sure whether donning the costume transforms the person into something else. By the end of this stage, the child may enjoy dressing up in costumes although he may still avoid face masks.

Differences between similar objects can be quantified or measured. He can see differences between the smallest and biggest (this is a big one, this is a baby one). However it is difficult for him to see a particular stick, placed in a row with other sticks from shorter to longer, as both longer than the stick to one side, and shorter than the one on the other side.

Knowing one way to group things (for example by size) may block another way of grouping them (for example by color).

The child can theorize about the world. He likes making guesses, and then trying out his hunches. He likes estimating. "Can you get all the toys in this box?" "Can you get your shirt on before I count to ten?"

His memory increases significantly. With a bit of practice, he remembers and can direct his parent as to the best route to take to the supermarket or to his friend's apartment.

His awareness of boundaries grows, including holding onto his perception of what is his. He wishes to extend this boundary considerably!

## Verbal Language Development

There is a vast increase in vocal expressions during this stage. Some basics of language are genetically programmed. Initially words are learned because they are paired with actions which occur in close temporal proximity to the words. Language acquisition is spurred on if the parents show interest in the child's vocalizations.

Rules of syntax appear and two or more words are combined in sentences. "Me do it." Words are used for identification (fire engine) and to indicate possession ("Doris teddy bear"). The child often refers to herself in the third person ("Patty do it").

The child can think of an object not immediately present and communicate with words about things not present. ("Mommy go work.") She uses language to learn about the world and tries things out in words. ("Rain come back?") This indicates she is beginning to be able to think in words, not just in actions. Verbal language becomes more reliable. ("Want some too much cake.")

Ability to understand and use verbal language develops rapidly during this stage. Receptive language far outstrips his ability to produce it. Reading stories at the level of his receptive language is therefore very important. The more language to which he is exposed, the better for his language development. Reliable research indicates an important correlation between exposure to verbal language and academic success in school.

The child is interested in opposites: big-small, rough-smooth, up-down, and yes-no—particularly *NO!* Word associations and thoughts become increasingly realistic although they may appear disassociated to adults. Visiting her grandfather who had completely recovered from a debilitating illness, Joan announced, "Grandpa backfired," meaning he was old (when he was ill) and then got young again (resumed his usual active state). Wanting to go to play with her friend across the street, she said, "Lets hoist go see Jenfeer," meaning "Pick me up and carry me to Jennifer's house."

The child understands only the literal meaning of words. Overhearing a conversation about mosquitos multiplying in standing water, David asked, "Water stands?"

Anna was helping her mother unpack a box of bulbs her mother had ordered. Her mother explained that they would plant the bulbs now, in the fall, and that in the spring they would have beautiful flowers in the garden. Anna dug through the wrapping material, pulled one of the bulbs out of the box, and held it out towards her mother with a look of total astonishment on her face, and exclaimed, "What this?!"

The only bulbs of which Anna had been aware were light bulbs. It had been interesting news to her, that light bulbs planted in the ground turned into flowers in the spring.

The child makes up words if she doesn't know the correct one. Mary identified all colors as being either blink or blurple. The child uses holistic speech—"cookie!" may stand for "I want a cookie."

The child uses over extensions—the word Daddy is used to refer to all men. Likewise the child uses under extensions—"cook" stands for "cookie."

A great deal of learning occurs by imitation and reinforcement of what is said by those around him. The color tone, phrasing, and pitch of the child's verbal language reflect the child's learning about social roles and situations. Having frequently heard adults exclaim, "Oh no," fifteen-month-old MacKay always used the expression with a tone of dismay, whenever she spotted something interesting.

The child carries on frequent long monologues, talking for her own enjoyment. She has no real interest in the response of the listener or in what the listener says in reply. She is simply enjoying her recently gained ability and skill with words. The meaning attached to words may change as the result of the child's experience. "Dog" carries a positive meaning until the child is nipped by a dog. "Dog" thereafter carries a negative meaning.

A bilingual child associates a particular language with the person who uses it with the child. Wishing him to be bilingual, Alejandro's parents only spoke Spanish to him for the first four years of his life. He was exposed to English outside the home. One day, when Alejandro was two years old, he and his mother were at a local playground. His mother asked an English speaking four-year-old playing nearby, how old he was. The child answered, "I'm four."

Since his Spanish-speaking mother had asked the question, Alejandro, wishing to join the conversation, added, referring to himself by his self-given nickname, "El nene tiene dos." (The baby is two).

"I," "me," and the child's name are used assertively. "Me do it myself! I not want! Marcus get down all self!" His ability to use affective expressions and communications vastly increases.

The child enjoys moving to music and by the end of this stage, attempts to sing along with songs which have a relatively simple melody and a repeating refrain. Songs which invite the child to move different parts of his body or imitate the sounds or movements of different animals are also enjoyed. He makes up songs he sings to himself.

The child can rather quickly be taught that snatching a toy from the child who was playing with it triggers an adult to scold, "That's not nice!" But what the child learns is not a morality lesson, but rather that his action will precipitate these nonsense words and then he will be separated from the toy that he has just snatched. He has learned that two things, snatching the toy and being removed from it, occur in close proximity in time.

Words unattached to a physical reality—for instance, moral connotations such as *should* and *should not* and *ought* that adults attach to words—simply do not make sense to the child. When two-year-old Margaret's father tells her she can't climb onto the table, she immediately tries to climb onto the table.

Margaret's father was using his words to indicate an abstract idea, that his daughter *ought not* climb onto the table, meaning that it was unacceptable for her to do so. However, the meaning Margaret attributes to her father's words is that her father thinks that she lacks the physical ability to climb onto the table so she hastens to disabuse him of his misperception.

Children's ability to understand and use verbal language develops rapidly from eighteen months of age to age five or six. For example, research indicates that a three-year-old may learn as many as eight hundred words in a single day.

## Physical Development

The child needs help dressing and undressing and with other daily tasks, even though he may demonstrate strong resentment of this fact. His appetite may fall off sharply at some point.

He gains control over his body's elimination functions, which he may exercise only when and where *he* chooses. Here are two tips concerning urination. If a male child doesn't wish to use the toilet, he may be quite willing to use any bushes available outside—or let him use a gallon sized plastic gallon size milk bottle which has had the neck cut off to widen the bottle's opening. He may be interested in standing on the rim of the toilet itself, trying to aim the stream of his urine at a wad of toilet paper which has been tossed into the bowl.

There are tremendous increases in the child's small and large muscle control, and in his eye-hand coordination. He can release objects gently as well as grasp and hold onto objects tightly.

His body is primarily vertical in shape, and he is steady on his feet. His stance conveys "Here I am. I am a person. I can do what I want to do. Me do it myself, no, you do it for me!"

He enjoys jumping, climbing, and throwing a ball, other objects, and himself with full physical force and abandon. If you need to entertain a two-year-old, ask the child to show you how high and for how long he can jump.

## Sensing and Feelings: Assessing Responsibility

The hallmark behavior of an upset two-year-old is shrieking "No!" before throwing himself down on the floor in a tantrum. He cannot yet experience and express middle ground feeling states and believes he is all powerful and capable of doing whatever he wants to do. When faced with the reality of the extent of his need for parental help, and thus his lack of omnipotence, he is overwhelmed with sadness and anger. It may be helpful to view tantrums as valuable opportunities for the child to *reset* emotionally.

Don't try to talk and reason with a child who is having a tantrum. Wait until the child has calmed down.

An important task during this time is to move from expression of the extremes of his feeling, to ability to express gradations of them. By the end of this stage he should be increasingly able to accept reality based limits which are imposed by adults on the expression of his feelings—and on occasion, set limits for himself on when, how, and to what extent he expresses his feelings.

It is helpful if the parents model appropriate expression of their own feelings—for instance, telling the child something that occurred at work or during a misunderstanding with a friend. The child needs to see how the parents handle their own feelings, particularly intense ones. At times the child will behave in ways that push the adult to intense feelings in order to have the parent model effective ways to manage such feelings.

The child experiences his feelings in actions. The parent needs to accept and return the child's affectionate outpourings and provide comfort and a physical haven for the child who is frightened. The parent should provide safe outlets for the child's physical expressions and communications of intensely experienced feelings. The child who is denied refuge or access to acceptable physical outlets for his intense feelings will believe he is being told that *having* such feelings is wrong and bad, and therefore that he is a wrong and bad person.

Children permitted to hit one another will conclude that the parents will not keep the children safe. A house rule permitting children to express their upset by hitting a soft object (a couch, a Blob) while a parent is in attendance is extremely helpful. A parent may say, "I can see by the way you are thrashing around on the Blob that you are really, really upset." This lets the child know that his feelings of upset are quite acceptable.

When a particular action of the child is found unacceptable, she experiences intense shame. She perceives that the whole person she is is unacceptable, and feels she has made a mess of her whole life. She wants to disappear and may try to escape from the situation by leaving—or by vociferously blaming someone else for the difficulty. During the next stage of development, the child will experience guilt, not shame, when an action of hers is found unacceptable. She will feel badly about what she has *done*, not badly about the whole person that she *is*.

## Making Decisions and Taking Action

The child needs to see that she can do things well, that she can please her parents. It is therefore very important for parents to comment on positive and pleasing actions the child takes. "I really *like* the way you ..." is more helpful than using a judgmental phrase such as "The way you ... was really *good*." Unfortunately, parents often forget to do affirm positive and pleasing actions, assuming that the child is aware that she has done the right thing. Parents tend only to comment on the child's unfortunate action choices.

The child needs to feel she has some strength and carries some weight in her environment, despite her limited size and capacity and ability to cope with events. It is essential that she is given opportunities to assert herself in acceptable ways—for example, in the choice of what she will wear or what toy she will take with her to the playground.

She is very interested in testing the relative power and strength of herself, others and objects in her environment. Bigger, stronger, more—these are the qualities that interest and impress the child most. The child throws her weight around in the family both physically and emotionally. Child and parent clash because, to the parent, it appears that the child wants to push the parent around, attack the parent personally, and make the parent's life generally miserable.

Remember that children ask questions with their behavior more often than with words. Their behavioral questions are experiments they are developmentally compelled to conduct. These experiments are conducted in order to discover how the world works, and where and what the limits are on a child's desire to run the world the way she'd like it to be.

Her questions have two parts. The first is content, in other words, "What will happen when I take this particular action?" The second is *procedural*: "To what extent do I have the power to have the world the way I want it to be?" Parents generally refer to this period of time as "the terrible twos."

The child fuels the fire of these clashes because she doesn't know which situations are appropriate for her assertions. In addition, she doesn't have control over gradations in her assertions, which most frequently are conducted with full emotional and physical force. Moreover, it is impossible for her to leave any room for negotiation before she acts, since thinking, feeling, and acting occur simultaneously.

Taking action is associated with the combined use of time and physical and social-emotional weight, or strength. In fact, accomplishing any task involves exerting some amount of strength in a certain amount of time. Intellectually, weight spans the range from taking something lightly to conveying that wild horses couldn't move the child from his or her position. On a physical level, weight spans the range of picking up a feather lightly to hurling a ball with full force.

The child is working on developing control over gradations of both kinds of weight (strength and power). This can only be accomplished by testing the amount of weight he or she has and is permitted to exert in different situations.

For example, here is the dialogue between two-year-old Katie and her father.

"It's almost time for you to get out of the hammock because we have to go home."

"I don't want to get out of the hammock."

"I know you don't. Take three more swings, and then it will be time to get out."

Katie takes more than three more swings.

"It's time to go now."

"I don't want to get out of the hammock."

"If you don't get out of the hammock by yourself, I will help you get out."

"I don't want you to help me get out of the hammock."

"I know you don't, but if you don't get out on your own, I will help you get out."

At this point a family friend who has been observing Katie and her father asks, "Katie, are you really big enough to get out of this hammock all by yourself?"

Katie shoots this adult a defiant look, proudly jumps out of the hammock, and struts to the door to go home with her father.

The child generally treats other children as objects which she views as more or less helpful. She doesn't consider the feelings of a child from whom she snatches a toy or the child she pushes out of her way, because she lacks sensory contact with their internal feelings. At this stage she only attributes the existence of feelings to herself, and, eventually during this stage, to her primary caretaker.

Two-year-old Lucile's interaction with her now two-month-old brother, Evan, had generally been positive, but she had inquired whether he was going to stay in her family "all the way until he got big." The mother placed a contented Evan in a nylon mesh port-a-crib in the living room, near where Lucile was happily playing with her stuffed toys. The mother, after going to the kitchen to prepare dinner, suddenly heard Evan shrieking. Hastening to the living room, the mother asked a smiling Lucile what had happened. Holding up her left hand, with fingers spread, Lucile poked the index finger of her right hand through the space between two of the fingers of her left hand and informed her mother matter of factly, "I poke he in the eye."

The precursors of intuition and true empathy are acquired during this stage by way of the responses the child receives to his or her actions.

By this age, the child's developing personality has been influenced and shaped by how he or she has been parented, and the way his or her family members have interacted with one another. For this reason, the child will at times *parent* a toy or another child as he or she has been parented, and may treat other children in the ways the child has been treated by the child's siblings.

The child has little understanding during this period that time is linear and is not reversible. Consider what happened between twenty-one-month-old Joe and his mother.

Joe's mother asked him if he wanted to finish the juice in his cup. Joe said he didn't want it. "If you don't want it, I'll drink it myself," said his mother. "Are you sure you don't want it?"

Joe shook his head and announced again, "No want it."

Joe's mother drank the remainder of the juice. Joe burst into tears, and collapsed on the floor, crying, "Do want! Do want!"

His mother picked him up to comfort him, saying, "I can get you some more juice if you want it."

"No!" wept the inconsolable Joe, trying to open his mother's mouth, "Want *that* juice (back)!"

Even when the child makes a positive and pleasing decision (I won't fuss about having to take a nap) and appears to understand physical time and demonstrates true empathy (social timing), the fact is that the child is making his action decision on the basis of his perception of the relative power possessed by the two people involved in the situation, himself and his mother. (Mom is bigger than I am so she will make me take a nap even if I fuss a whole lot so I might just as well give in.)

Delivering a verbal lesson on morally appropriate behavior has no meaning to a child of this age. The child cannot understand the abstract concepts of right and wrong, should and ought.

It is best for the parent to give one warning when unacceptable behavior occurs. If the behavior continues, the parent should take an action which physically prevents the child from repeating the unacceptable behavior. The intervention needs to convey the parent's ability to channel his own thoughts and feelings into appropriate actions. This is much easier to accomplish if intervention is made well before the parent's emotional state borders on feeling or being out of control.

Parents are often concerned about being consistent in their reaction to a child's unacceptable behavior. Here are some things to keep in mind when choosing an appropriate response to the child's unacceptable actions:

Keep the focus just on the immediate situation, not on what has occurred in the past. For example, "We're finished with the sandbox for today because throwing sand doesn't work for me," rather than "I'm sick of always having trouble at the sandbox."

Focus on taking steps which will improve your own mood, and that of all those affected by the situation. For instance, "I have a headache, so the toy police cars and fire engines with sirens will have to be used in another room." rather than "Get those screaming vehicles out of here right now; the noise is driving me crazy!"

Acknowledge the child's right to think and feel the way she does. Your response should only be concerned with her unfortunate action decision. For example, "I understand that you're very angry with the dog because he ate your cookie, but I won't let the dog be hit."

Some children are very sensitive to a disapproving tone of voice, and respond to it by correcting their behavior, while others require action on the part of the parent. For example, the following statements can be said in a way that indicates strong disappointment: "Making a collage is fine, but I really don't want to see glue on the table. Glue belongs on the paper."

Pairing a few explanatory words with a physical response reinforces the meaning and importance of verbal communication. For instance, when two-year-old Lily hit her brother, her mother picked her up and said, "I will not let one of my children hit another of my children." The mother removed Lily without further discussion, while commenting in a neutral tone of voice, "Keeping both of my children safe is an important job for a mother. So, I am going to put the hitting child and the child who was hit in separate rooms for a while."

It is possible to ameliorate a bad situation by providing the child with a safe place and object to physically express the extent of his upset. Encourage the child to pound away on the object, pinch it harder, jump on it longer, pommel it with more and more force. Complimenting the child on his ability to show you how upset he is keeps you in conversational contact with the child. Eventually, lactic acid will build up in the child's muscles to the point of exhaustion and the child will relax. When this point is reached, the child, and you, will be on the way to a better mood.

Advance notice and preparation for a transition between activities will help develop in the child an internalized sense of time. Give the child something to hold on to during the transition. For example, "Hold on to your doll, we are getting ready to get into the car in a couple of minutes, and I know you want to have her with you." Or, instead of asking a tired child to simply walk out of the playground, introduce an imaginative angle. For example, "Let's sneak out of the park, so no one even knows we're leaving."

## Family Life

In conducting family life, a major concern of the parents needs to be providing a balanced allocation of attention, energy, and resources to adequately meet the needs of each family member. This encourages the child to choose, by the end of this stage, realistic rather than fantasied perceptions about his place and importance in the world.

Many, if not most, parents are pressed for time to address essential tasks of the week, and achieving the balanced life described above seems an impossible goal to *contemplate*, let alone *achieve*. What is more possible to arrange is a rotation of times when particular attention is set aside, for both individual and different combinations of family members.

Excluding a child from important adult conversations ("If you interrupt us, we will make sure you are safe, but you will not be allowed in the room with us until we are finished talking.") is as important as providing regularly occurring Special Time.

Behavioral limits need to be stated clearly and impersonally, including what actions are acceptable, as well as which are not. Removing an out-of-control shrieking child to a safe "screaming place" to recover can be helpful. I strongly recommend Hiam Ginott's book, *Between Parent and Child* for straightforward, effective setting and enforcing of behavioral limits.

Hearing adults recount emotionally significant events in their own daily lives speaks to the child's need to learn what causes different feeling states and how to manage them. It is also helpful to review the child's day with him or her, including naming feelings you *think* the child experienced. However, be prepared to accept it if the child doesn't agree with you. For example, the child may not agree with your statement, "*I* think you were sad when your friend Steven had to go home."

The child's actions need to be recognized as assertions and expressions of himself, not as aggressions against others. Try to make space for partial satisfaction for the child's desire. For example, giving the child permission to explore his or her own body in private (but not in the presence of others).

Since the child is just acquiring an understanding of the way things really are, significant changes in family life at this time may be particularly upsetting. The child needs reassurance about how important events in his everyday life will proceed and how contact with significant people and with his important belongings will continue to occur.

Being *fair* doesn't necessarily mean doing the same thing for everyone involved. Acknowledge the child's perception of unfairness in situations, and point out that the child will be getting something he wants in a short time. For example, "I know it's hard for you play by yourself right now because I have to feed the baby. But the baby is too young to listen to stories, so she will have to take a nap after I feed her and just you and I will read together."

## Activities

Children play for different reasons: for entertainment; for mastery of a skill (building a high tower with building blocks); to change the outcome of an unhappy event (throwing his teddy bear out of his room after he was denied access to the room in which his father and brother were assembling a complicated model airplane on the floor); or to mirror what the child has observed occurring between people in her environment (wrapping a stuffed toy needing comfort in a blanket and rocking it).

Children make numerous mistakes in a day. Providing materials which allow them to *mess up* with impunity encourages willingness to *risk* offering answers to academic questions posed later at school, and to take reasonable risks in other areas of life. Puddings make fine edible finger-paint on a plate or placemat. Shaving cream (regular, not mentholated) makes a clean mess which allows the child to *mess up* the sink, bathtub, placemat, table, or themselves. Even rubbed into clothes, it disappears in minutes and leaves no trace.

The child generally attends to his own play *in the presence of* other children who are also playing, rather than *playing with* the other children. The child shares toys with strong adult support, but relates to other children as objects which are more or less helpful. By the end of this stage, the child begins to relate to one or two important people in his life as people with whom he can play cooperatively. This only occurs with dawning recognition that others have feelings, just as he does, which need to be considered.

The child enjoys playing hide and seek with his parent. He hides but then watches (often in clear sight of the parent) while the parent looks for him. The child enjoys this game because he is the one who arranges the reunion with the adult.

He likes playing "baby" but this should be done when he is generally acting in an age-appropriate way, not when he is acting like a much younger child. Playing "baby" helps the child accept that time is only reversible in fantasy or play.

Create opportunities for jumping: from the front door to the sidewalk; from sidewalk square to sidewalk square; from the bottom step of the porch leading up to a house; across an "island" (the living room rug).

Let the child darken colored objects outside with a small, thin-handled paintbrush and a small container of water.

Fill the kitchen sink with warm water, and let the child stand on a chair to play with objects in the sink. This can be varied to keep it interesting. For example, put different types of toys in the sink on different occasions—doll house contents, toy vehicles, kitchen utensils like soup ladles, slotted spoons, and measuring spoons. Give the child containers of different sizes to encourage experiments with measuring and volume. Add soap bubbles or a few drops of food coloring to the water. Let the child use a small tea strainer, or make a shower out of a plastic container by poking holes in the bottom of it with a nail.

Have the child sort three types of dry cereal you have combined in a large bowl into three separate containers. After sorting, the child is welcome to eat them all. If it is too enticing to see, and not eat the food during sorting, give the child a combination of three types of cereal and ask him or her to choose and eat only one type of cereal. When that has been consumed, move on to another type of cereal.

Be sure to treat the child's cereal "mistakes" with good humor, not condemnation. For instance, asking lightheartedly, "Is that a toasted o?" when the child has just eaten a totally different brand name cereal.

Take turns with the child, pretending to move or to sound like different animals. Guess which animal is being imitated.

Toys and building sets made of interlocking plastic pieces are of endless interest, particularly if they are stored in their own containers and not mixed in with other toys.

Make "houses" out of cardboard home appliance boxes (obtainable from a store that sells kitchen appliances). Cut out windows and a door, and let the child play inside the "house." A second room can be added by attaching a second carton with duct tape. Let the child decorate the walls with crayons, magic markers, or water-based paint.

Have daily reading times with the child, during which you vary your voice as the narrative indicates, and ask the child questions about the stories.

Have the child help you by dumping pre-measured ingredients for cookie dough into a bowl and then mixing the ingredients together with his hands.

Let the child string beads or plastic straws (cut into one-inch lengths) onto a long shoelace (tie one bead onto an end of the shoelace to keep the beads from slipping off that end), or string pieces of macaroni of different sizes and shapes.

Have a couple sets of blocks of different sizes with which the child can play, each set stored in its own container.

Make collages by gluing differently sized and shaped pieces of paper, bottle caps, styrofoam peanuts, leaves collected on a walk, etc., onto pieces of cardboard.

Children enjoy activities that involve identifying and moving their own body parts—large motions using the whole body, jumping, throwing objects down with force and loud sounds. Remember that the child is interested in big and bigger actions, sounds, and things.

Scrunching up pieces of paper and throwing them into the waste basket as hard as he can is fun. So is punching the Blob, a mattress or a couch with all his strength, to show the parent or other adult how strong he is becoming.

## Self-Image – If All Goes Well Enough

The child believes he or she is a *good enough*, a sufficiently powerful male or female in his or her environment. She perceives sufficient support and opportunity to safely express her often intense and negative thoughts and feelings in actions. Therefore, she doesn't have to resort to fantasy to boost her self-esteem, believing that she is powerful enough in real life to deal with the situation at hand. She recognizes that just because she wants it to be so doesn't make it so.

She accepts herself and believes she is acceptable to others, even though she frequently feels like building things up and tearing them down. She wants to do for herself one minute and wants others to do for her the next. She often messes up, throws her weight around, and has her wishes totally ignored or overruled a number of times in a day. She expresses and communicates her feelings more and more frequently in intensity and amounts appropriate to the situation at hand.

She has increasing tolerance for simultaneously experiencing intensely felt, opposing emotions, and her focus is often on *doing* something about a situation, not just on venting her intensely felt emotions.

She is more frequently focused on discharging her own responsibilities rather than focusing on the justice or injustice in the apportionment of tasks, or the potential reward. She can both lead and follow, and with adult help she can accept transitions between these two roles.

Her increased reality testing ability allows her to understand that people react to her positive and negative actions rather than to her motivation. Before achieving this ability she would say, "It's your fault that I broke the glass because you told me to carry it." Now, at least with adult support, she can sometimes admit that the glass broke because she dropped it.

She uses words to communicate her positive and negative thoughts and feelings. She recognizes that words have common meaning. For example, when asked, she accurately names the different colors of magic markers, rather than being satisfied with identifying them the way she used to, with made up words like blink or blurple.

## Difficulties Linked to This Stage That May Emerge Later

He may have difficulty realistically assessing his own power in situations. For example, as a student, he may consider it his responsibility to tell his teacher about the misbehavior of his classmates which occurred while the teacher was out of the classroom, which is likely to negatively impact his relationship with classmates.

He may have difficulty acknowledging the feelings he has to others, and to himself and may refrain from taking appropriate actions in honor of his feelings. For example, he may not acknowledge to himself sadness at a significant loss, or may refuse to acknowledge responsibility for his negative feelings and/or actions, even though they may be quite evident to others.

Rather than realizing that some of his feelings are unacceptable to himself, he may attribute them to another, and condemn their presence in that other person. He may claim to have the opposite feeling from the one he really has. For example, "I *never* get mad at my spouse, I *love* my spouse." He may have a difficult time tolerating ambivalent feelings in others. For example, when his friend says, "I love my spouse, but at times, I really get angry with her." He may be overly concerned with fairness and follow the letter rather than considering the spirit of the law or considering all aspects of the particular situation.

His fear of making mistakes—of "messing up"—may cause him to avoid taking even insignificant risks, such as volunteering to answer a question posed by a teacher, or trying out a new sport. His focus is on potential judgment on his performance or that of others, rather than on participation in an activity.

If he cheats and is found out, he is upset because he was caught, not because he did the wrong thing.

He may have difficulty asserting his own needs and wishes. He doesn't say, "I'd like you to get it for me now." Instead, he may be *passive*, say nothing and get whatever it is himself, but later he expects/demands some *payment* for his poor, martyred existence. Thus he lends credence to the saying, "I'll tell you now, or I'll get you later." Or he may inappropriately aggressively *demand* that another do something for him.

He does not feel sadness or guilt when he *messes up* and makes a mistake. Instead, he experiences shame, finding his entire self to be a *mess up*. He does not focus on finding a realistic way to rectify the situation. Instead, his focus is on fleeing the experience of shame. He may physically leave the situation abruptly; end an entire relationship with a person; attempt to mentally escape by deadening perceptions of his feelings by temporarily disassociating from them, or he may take actions which are not in his best interest, which provide some proof to himself, and possibly to others, that he is indeed "a total mess up."

# Three to Six Years of Age
## Chapter 5

### Use of Energy

During three to five years of age the child focuses on the ability to take an ever increasing number and range of actions on his or her own and in cooperation with others. In order to learn on an intellectual, physical, and emotional level, the child needs a wide range of opportunities to operate physically in and on his environment. The more such opportunities the child has, the greater his chances to improve abstract thinking, which begins to develop somewhere between nine and eleven years of age.

It is a major concern that much of the physical experimentation historically available during childhood has been replaced by involvement with two-dimensional electronic devices (smart phones, tablets, computers, TV, etc.). Additionally, the extended involvement of both parents and children with devices means that less of the parents' attention is given to being emotionally present with the child, and fewer opportunities for the child to be present during more extensive direct verbal contact between older children and significant adults in their lives.

### Thinking, Paying Attention, and Learning

There are crucial changes in the child's thinking. Most important of all, the child now thinks and attributes meaning to internal and external events as the adult does, in words. This vastly improves chances of clear communication between child and adult.

At this point it would be extremely confusing to the child to continue to think in the nonverbal language he has relied on until now. For example, when angry with his parents, the child no longer wants to bite them and eat them up as he did previously; nor does he fear they want to destroy him in like manner.

Such confusion is avoided by a one-time, comprehensive banishment from his conscious mind of the child's previous way of thinking, along with almost all memory that he had in fact *ever* thought that way. This greatly facilitates the child's effective and efficient functioning. However, as discussed elsewhere in this writing, what he learned and stored during his previous way of thinking does not vanish. It continues to reside in his *less than conscious mind*, and continues to exert significant influence on choices he makes about how his important relationships with others are to be conducted.

Although the child now thinks in words, there are still significant differences in the way he thinks, compared to the way adults think. Here are some examples:

Some magical thinking is still present in this stage; an object is as alive as a person. The child accepts an explanation given to him, puts it into human terms, and adds his own fantasy elements to it. Having been told there isn't a heat source on the moon, five-year-old Martha told her mother to "Leave the window open so the moon can get his scarf if he gets cold." Tell a four-year-old who loves dinosaurs that one is really coming down the street and he will turn to see if it is there. A six-year-old will laugh and say, "You're kidding me!"

The child thinks only about things in the present, although he is conscious that some things existed before he and before his parents were present. In a discussion with four- and five-year-olds about things which are here now and things which are no longer here, one child asked, "Are there still dinosaurs?" Another child quickly jumped in and said, "No, they're not here anymore—cars killed them."

The child's conscience (his internalized sense of right and wrong) is developing during this stage. How guilty he feels about his actions, however, depends on the amount of damage that occurs ("I only took one cookie!") rather than because he feels badly about his action. An older child feels badly when he takes something that isn't his; how many he takes would be of secondary importance.

The child has a highly active imagination and may have imaginary playmates. This should not be discouraged. A friend arrived at our house with her four-year-old son, Steven. She confided in me that Steven had an imaginary friend. I could see that she was wondering if this was a normal occurrence. I told her that I thought it was quite normal, but that David (my son) didn't happen to have one.

She and I were standing at the foot of the first floor staircase in our house. At that precise moment, David appeared at the top of the stairs, turned to no one *we* could see, and said, "Come on, Stuart," and bounced down the stairs to play with Steven.

Steven's mother gave me a look that conveyed disgust at what she perceived as my unwillingness to acknowledge that my child also had an imaginary friend. As it happened, that was the one and only time I ever heard my son refer to an imaginary friend!

An internalized sense of time begins to develop. By six years of age, acceptance of the linearity and irreversibility of time is set. In my experience, this seems to result in one or two months during which the child appears to be in a somewhat somber mood, which can't be tied to any particular event or situation in his life. The child rebounds on his own, without any outside assistance.

Absence of awareness that time moves in only one direction is clearly evident in the thinking of the three-year-old. Ask one how big her parents will be when *she* is a grown up, and she will tell you that they will be little, as she is now. A six-year-old will laugh and say, "Silly! They will be the same size as they are now!"

Once the child understands that time is linear and nonreversible, his upset when exposed to the death of a loved person or animal increases. And since the child believes that he has a causal part in whatever he experiences, he worries when a loved one dies. It's a good idea to ask if and what the child thinks he might have done to cause the loss.

Three-year-old Nathan encountered a piano for the first time at the home of friends of his parents. He spent a long time happily discovering what sounds he could elicit from the instrument, and pitched a grand fit when told that it was time to go home. However, when informed that the piano would stay right where it was until Nathan returned for another visit, he easily said good bye to the piano, and walked out the door to the family car.

From experience, Nathan knew that brief absences from his parents, and his favorite blanket (removed for laundering), were followed by reunion with them. He needed reassurance that reunion with this *new* object would also occur in what, for him, would be a manageable amount of time.

The child seeks knowledge of himself, others, the world, and of the relationships between these entities. He pursues this knowledge by asking questions, as mentioned above, and by experimenting on and with people, objects, and materials. He can grasp cause and effect on a concrete level, and his problem-solving ability increases. He invents and makes discoveries, through sensory experimentation, and then enjoys telling people about his discoveries.

He is interested first and foremost in the animate world, because he can see it move. Only later does his interest in inanimate objects like the sun and stars appear. He is interested in classification (animals which fly, machines which dig) and quantification (how many marbles will fit in this container). These interests reflect preparation for the reasoning needed in the early elementary school years.

He has difficulty with relationships occurring in more than one direction, saying to his mom, "I'm your baby, so you can't be the baby of my grandma."

He is intermittently able to make room for different views on a subject and to switch between points of view. Eventually he is able to simultaneously focus on several views, which allows the possibility of real discussions.

He judges things on their present state, not how they came to be. An example of this is the lack of what Piaget called "conservation of volume." He will be sure the tall glass has more liquid in in than the short glass, even if he saw the same amount of liquid poured into the two glasses.

Even when the child seems to be asking about causality, she is really interested in the psycho-moral determinants of the event. She can't yet distinguish between mental, physical, or social reality or between moral and physical laws. Therefore, give the child functional answers—i.e. corn grows so we can have cereal in the morning; we have to go to bed at night because night time is for sleeping; leaves fall to cover the grass during the winter.

She shows a preference for learning and committing information to memory either visually, kinesthetically, or aurally. She believes in the sanctity of rules, although she can't follow them very well at all.

She doesn't understand space, time, or number concepts beyond ten, although she may be able to count far beyond ten. The teacher at a kindergarten readiness interview wanted to see if Indigo could count to twenty, one of the school's benchmarks for readiness. The teacher asked how high Indigo could count. Indigo answered that she could count to one hundred, but explained that it would take a long time.

The child can only focus on one physical aspect, or dimension, of an object, situation, or person at a time. Answering the question, "Are there more red or yellow wooden blocks?" is difficult.

She is able to remember in sequence and detail things she has experienced. However, recalling unrelated items she has seen some time ago is difficult.

Memory and sequencing games are important. In the game of concentration, cards are placed, face down, on the table, in a grid. Each player can turn over two cards when it is her turn, hoping to find two which have matching faces. If they match, the player keeps the cards. If not, the two cards are replaced, face down, and the next player has a turn. This can be adapted to the age of the child by controlling the number of cards used.

Another such game involves an adult and a child taking turns, silently watching as one person touches three different objects, while slowly moving about in the room. The observer then tries to touch those three objects in the same sequence. This game may be played with the repetition of three words, or sounds animals make, or by moving in three different ways—for example: jump, clap your hands together, shake your head. Insist that the movements used by you and the child are simple enough for you to follow.

## Language Development and Music Development

### Language Development

First, his vocabulary, already vast, continues to expand daily. Second, by the end of this stage, the child's verbal language becomes reliable. For example, he says he really, really *wants* a pony for his birthday. However (unlike a younger child who thinks that wishing influences events), he realizes that because he lives in a high-rise apartment, this won't happen. Third, the child is aware that words sometimes have more than a literal meaning. For example, he understands his mother is feeling overwhelmed when she says, "I'm up to my ears in paperwork!"

Research demonstrates that exposure to verbal language at this stage directly increases the child's later academic performance. He learns up to eight hundred words a day. Although ability to use verbal language grows by leaps and bounds, it is far outdistanced by his receptive language ability. It is very important, therefore, to read stories to the child that are on his comprehension level. He likes stories about what people do in different places, both familiar and unfamiliar to the child. He like stories about different occupations, about how things work, and where things are (under the street, in the ocean).

Although still learning by taking action, she uses full sentences. She desires real conversations with other children and adults. She can repeat short nursery rhymes and she makes up her own stories. Her talking may be almost constant, partly to be in contact with others, partly because she takes pleasure in the number and variety of words she can produce and use.

The hallmark language activity of this stage is asking unending streams of questions. The only way to stop a particular stream of questions is to ask the child what he thinks the answer to the question is and why he thinks this is so. This may provide a brief respite before the next stream of questions begins. This is the verbal equivalent of the hallmark physical activity of this stage. Once running, the three-year-old can be stopped only by an immovable barrier. The child demonstrates readiness for kindergarten when, told to stop running just before reaching a chain link fence, he applies internal brakes and manages to stop.

Remember that there are two parts to the child's questions. The child seeks particular information (the *content* of the question) and tries to discover how many questions he will be permitted to ask at that particular time (the *procedural* part of the question). Therefore, parents need not fear firmly setting limits on the number of questions they will answer on an occasion. They will soon be asked to answer more. The child believes that parents know the answers to all questions, and is very surprised to learn that this is not the case.

The child enjoys playing with language. Hearing an adult conversation about San Diego, he may interject, "Eggs aren't sandy!" and laugh. When the child has mastered elimination functions, talking and laughing about them becomes very enjoyable. Just saying "poop" can set off gales of laughter. By the time the child is five years old, he may refrain from acting in such an undignified manner. However, taunts indicating "I have it and you don't," or "I can and you can't," are still vastly entertaining.

## Music Development

The child can think, sing, and move simultaneously. Children's circle games are quite enjoyable for this reason—for example, "Old MacDonald Had A Farm" and "Ring Around The Rosie." She sings for her own pleasure and can keep a beat. Songs which tell stories and have accompanying movements are of great interest—for instance, "The Fox Went Out On A Chilly Night," "My Darling Clementine," and "She'll be Coming Round The Mountain."

Songs which present problems, like "What shall We Do With The Drunken Sailor" are intriguing, if followed by a discussion of what the child might do to solve the problem the song presents. For instance, if we throw the drunken sailor overboard, we will have to do his job for the remainder of the trip, so we need to think of a consequence which will inspire him to do his job, not end his life or permanently incapacitate him.

Songs which have many verses, or involve sequencing speak to the child's interest in time—for example, "I Know An Old Lady Who Swallowed A Fly." Songs and games which encourage the child to makes the sounds or movements of different categories of things (animals in the water, sky, or ground) are also enjoyed.

## Sensing and Feelings: Assessing Responsibility

The child's comfort with expressing and communicating the full range of all four types of feelings (happy, sad, angry, scared) increases by leaps and bounds during this stage. Creative activities, fantasy play on his own and with other children, and conversations with parents and other adults help the child manage his feelings in acceptable ways, even when they are intensely experienced.

Here is an example of how five-year-old Bethany expressed her intense upset and clearly communicated its gradual dissipation in her creative expressions. Bethany's parents had separated and planned to divorce. Bethany continued to behave well most of the time, both at home and at school. However, Bethany was a prolific artist and tears flowed from all of the objects in the numerous pictures she drew and painted.

Her teacher and parents thought it would be helpful if Bethany talked with the school counselor. In their first conversation, Bethany acknowledged that she was "a little sad" that her parents didn't live together, but she spent most of her time in the counselor's office playing with the toys. Just before Bethany left the room, she reached down, appeared to be opening a small, imaginary door in the floor. She threw two imaginary objects through the imaginary opening in the floor. Then she slammed the imaginary door shut with a look of satisfaction, and headed out of the office.

The counselor asked if she could say something about what she had just done. "Well," explained Bethany, "I put my parents into the washing machine because they don't read me bedtime stories anymore!"

Over the next two months the counselor met with Bethany's parents twice and met with Bethany once every week. At the end of each meeting, the counselor asked Bethany if she was ready to take her parents out of the washing machine yet. Bethany would then open the *door* of the washing machine, peer in and declare, "Nope!" At the start of the eighth meeting Bethany, without any prompting, walked over to the imaginary door, opened the washing machine, took both parents out, and announced, "They're reading me stories again." From then on, tears no longer flowed from her artistic creations.

The child believes that inanimate objects, like people, have feelings. One day young Albert went to use the toilet in a department store men's room. No one else was in the bathroom at that time. When he returned to his mother, he asked, "Do toilets have feelings?" His mother replied, "No, they don't have feelings as people do." After a pause, Albert said, "Ugh! What if they could taste!"

Abstract thinking is still absent in this stage, so the child still searches for the physical location and cause of feelings. One day five-year-old Jenny's mother was very grumpy with Jenny. Jenny looked for a way to get rid of her mother's grumpiness. The next day, her mother found the gray sweatshirt she (the mother) had been wearing the previous day, stuffed behind one radiator. She asked Jenny if she had put it there. "Yes," said Jenny, "I wanted to throw it away." "You didn't like my grumpiness yesterday, did you?" her mother asked. "No," said Jenny.

Four-year-old Claire's mother had repeatedly soothed Claire's fears with explanations and accompanying comforting actions. Her mother had just finished adding claws to a pair of Claire's mittens, for Claire to wear as part of a dinosaur costume needed for the nursery school play. Claire tried the mittens on, and then, fearing her mother might be frightened, Claire explained, "You can't touch them (the claws)." In a comforting tone, she added, "See what's underneath? Look …" She withdrew her hand from the mitten. "You can touch this; it's my hand."

Fears tend to appear around four years of age, especially at night. There are a number of books on the subject which can be very helpful. Giving the child a flashlight to shine on any possible monsters or a spray bottle filled with water may help (it is generally accepted that monsters and such leave the premises wherever there is light or water).

Parents need to be careful to not inadvertently feed the child's fears. Letting the child gain admittance to the parents' bed in response to the child's nighttime fears may lead the child to two unfortunate assumptions. Each assumption can lead to further difficulties.

The first is that it confirms that there *is indeed* something to fear in the child's room—why else would the parents think the child should sleep elsewhere? The second is that since the parents and the child sleep in the same place, they do have or should have equal power. This may lead the child to vehemently object to parental requirements placed on him during the day.

These misunderstandings can be avoided if the parent goes to the child's room to provide comfort, sitting beside the child's bed, conveying that it is safe for the child to sleep by himself in his own bed.

One mother always welcomed her frightened child into her bed, helping the child settle cozily under the covers. Then the mother, feigning sleep, would begin to move and thrash about and grab up the covers in such a way that the child was quite uncomfortable. The child soon retreated, of his own volition, to his own bed.

When angry with another person, children, *like adults*, prefer to think that the other party is at fault. Children need adult support to keep the focus on the problem, rather than on announcing blame, and to recognize that everyone involved in a conflict shares responsibility for its occurrence. When facilitating a conversation between two (or more) children who are angry with each other, it is worth the effort to require that each disputant talk only about himself.

First (as previously discussed), insist that statements made by either child be restated as "I" statements which do not contain the word "you." For example, the accusation "You hit me when I was still swinging" becomes "I got hit when I was still swinging."

Next, ask each child to state his feelings about what happened. You, the parent, should acknowledge the feelings of each person involved in the dispute. For example, one child says, "I was mad, up to the roof, when I didn't get my turn." "Yes," you might say, "It is very annoying not to get your turn."

Finally, either tell the children what is going to happen to improve the situation, or ask them for suggestions of steps to take to resolve the conflict. Talk about how to avoid such a situation in the future.

Consider having a family rule that both *victim* and *aggressor* may be held responsible for their respective behavior: the aggressor for taking a physical action against the victim; and the victim, if the parent believes he could have kept himself safe by leaving the situation sooner and seeking adult help.

Parents frequently fail to realize that their young child continues to rely, to an important extent, on his or her first language of nonverbal behavior. Consequently, parents often refrain from speaking about significant difficulty they are having with each other in the presence of their child in order to protect the child from such knowledge. However, the young child accurately interprets the meaning of the nonverbal behavior occurring between his parents.

Asking the child, out of the presence of his parents, a *comparative* question about *how much trouble* the child thinks the parents are having, and what he *thinks might happen*, usually reveals how much the child knows about his parents' situation. An example of such a question is "Do you think your parents are having a little, medium, or big trouble with each other?" A straightforward question, such as, "Do you think your parents are having trouble with each other?" elicits less information. Be careful not to argue with the child's report. If it doesn't match your own assessment, just verbally acknowledge that you and the child have different ideas about the relationship between the parents.

If a major change in the family is planned, such as a separation or divorce, or if there is significant illness in a family member, conversations should be held with the child, as the situation develops. In these conversations child and adult can share feelings each has, and the child can be offered reassurance in a way appropriate to his developmental age, about how his needs will be met, regardless of changes in the family situation. More will be said about handling such changes in the family, in the section covering six years of age to puberty.

## Physical Development

The child's body shape is vertical, but with a bulging stomach. Think of the Kewpie Doll stance. Increased control in small and large muscles results in more efficient manipulation of materials and greater participation in a wide range of activities. Her balance is good, and she tries to tie her shoes. She builds towers and complex structures with blocks, throws a ball overhead, draws and paints pictures with more control. She starts to form letters, can cut with scissors, and handle glue and different types of tape with increasing facility.

She can accommodate her body shape and activity to available physical space, and can share a small space with another. This is empathic cooperation on a physical level. She can mirror the movement of others ("Simon Says" or "The Hokey Pokey") and design creative movement stunts and tricks on her own and cooperatively. She enjoys having adults watch her perform.

Running is a preferred activity. At three, she runs and runs until stopped by an unyielding barrier. At five, she can control and curb her momentum before reaching the barrier. Responding to changing circumstances, she can move with gradations of speed from quickness to a leisurely pace. Generally speaking, faster is much more attractive to her than moving with slow concentration and deliberation. She can act with varying degrees of force, from extreme strength to light touch, and can restrict, or freely use her physical energy, depending on the particular activity.

Parental response to the child's sensuality and sexuality strongly impacts the child. Sex education starts with the parents' own attitudes about sensuality and sexuality. Clear messages about both are conveyed by sleeping arrangements, the quantity and emotional tenor of physical contact between the parents, and reaction to the child's sexual curiosity and experimentation.

It can be difficult for parents to be pleased when the child says, or the parent discovers, that the child experiences genital pleasure, even though this is a developmentally positive sign.

Proximity of elimination and sexual organs encourages the child to experiment and experience. Remember, the child is well aware of the frequent attention that her parents have paid to that area (in bathing and diaper changing). Parents need to recognize the child's curiosity, but focus on letting the child know the proper time and place for such activity, including the need for privacy.

Parents should continue to allow activities in which *messing up* is encouraged—for example, playing with shaving cream, or building and knocking down block structures, or heaving water filled balloons. This is not unrelated to sexuality. Adults often refer to sexual activity as "messing around." The idea is to provide the child with a variety of activities which allow acceptable *messing around* in social settings.

## Making Decisions and Taking Actions

Since it is impossible to take every action at once, prioritizing, sequencing, and choosing which action to take become essential organizational skills. These skills require an internalized sense of the passing of physical time and an internalized sense of social timing/empathy. By the end of this stage, adequate organizational skills are established, although adult support will be needed as the skills are practiced.

Time-related difficulties are still handled on a concrete level. Five-year-old Paul's mother was late to pick him from school. Said Paul, "I'm going to give you all of my clocks, so that you won't forget what time it is."

The child usually has a schema for the sequence of events which regularly repeat in time, such as bedtime routines. Changes in such routines will be accepted on some nights, but vigorously objected to on others, with the child proclaiming, "That's not how bedtime happens!"

Activities which allow the child himself to help to create changes over time are of particular interest. These include cooking, planting seeds, making and using play dough, and using woodworking tools. Activities involving speed are also of particular interest. Toys will be put away with more enthusiasm if the child is asked to work against a deadline. For example, "Do you think you can get all of these toys put away by the time I finish washing the dishes?" usually works better than "It's time to clean up the toys."

The child's ability to operate electronic devices may well astound his parents. It is essential, however, that the preponderance of the child's activity time not be spent with such equipment, but rather in activities involving his entire body. Athletic activities are important, as long as they do not involve competition. Remember that the young child who "strikes out" in a baseball game will still perceive his entire self to be a *strike out*.

The child can sometimes plan, prepare for a task, carry through on it, clean up, recuperate from that task, and make a reasonably good transition to the next activity with minimal adult supervision. This sequence is facilitated by use of a repeating rhythmic chant to announce the start of a new activity or the approaching end of an activity. For example, "Now it's time to clean up, clean up, clean up, now it's time to clean up all the toys." Or, "Soon we're going to go outside, go outside, go outside …," etc.

In creative play the child tries out different perspectives, roles, actions, and feeling sequences. She can practice what she already knows about the external world, and can express and communicate about her interior life in safe, socially acceptable ways. She does this through activities such as drawing, painting, sculpting; constructing houses and towns with blocks and vehicles; making things with wood and tools, and in dress-up play. She can vent her intense feelings in such activities, rather than visiting those feelings directly on people. For example, she can hammer on wood rather than hammering on her brother. The child is working on making decisions about how and when to act on her thoughts and feelings. A younger child expresses what she thinks and feels in rather immediate actions. By contrast, a child approaching age five may well say to another, "You want to play with the doll that I have, so I will let you play with it for two minutes, and then you give it right back to me, okay?"

He tries to be responsible, and his interaction with other children is generally peaceful and cooperative, although adult support is needed to help manage moments of conflict. The child may have a best friend for a time, and then may choose a different best friend. He may want to play exclusively with his current best friend.

## Family Life

Setting and enforcing generational boundaries is an important part of the endeavor to create a reasonable balance in meeting the disparate needs and wishes of all family members. This includes setting aside time for adults to have private time to enjoy one another's company. The child can to be told that when grown up, he can find a partner of his own but that right now, the parents belong to each other, and therefore get to spend private time with each other, away from children.

Parents need to set realistic and specific demands for the child's behavior in specific situations, and look for opportunities to appreciate his or her increasing skills. For example, "I can see how much better you are now at scrubbing your teeth than you used to be."

Be specific about changes you need to see in the child's behavior—for instance, "I need to see teeth being scrubbed, not the toothbrush being flown around like an airplane." Saying, "I see some toys are still on the floor. When I come back in five minutes I want to see that all of the toys are in the toy box" allows the child opportunity to be thanked for doing the right thing.

Verbalize the connection between your behavioral demands and the reason for them. For instance, say "I may trip and hurt myself if toys are left all over the floor," rather than "Do it because I'm the parent and I say so!"

If emotions are running high (in parent, child, or both) try to get through the immediate situation as best you can, and talk about it when the atmosphere is calmer.

Although the child tries to observe physical and social time limits, at times this is difficult. For instance, parents complain that their child frequently interrupts their adult conversations. These interruptions can be reduced if a few steps are taken:

1. Tell the child that you are available to help him for a few minutes now if he needs something, and then you will be unavailable until your adult conversation is over.

2. Set a timer for the amount of time you will be unavailable. An analog timer allows the child to determine (by eye and ear) time passing. Tell the child he is not to interrupt you until the timer's bell rings.

3. If you wish, you may give the child the option to play quietly by himself in the room with you, as long as your conversation is not interrupted. Then begin your conversation. If interrupted, calmly remove the child from the room and say, "I see you have chosen to play in the other room while the adults talk. I can see you're not happy with your choice, but you will have a chance to make a different choice on another day when I am having a conversation."

4. If the child is otherwise occupied when the bell of the timer rings, enjoy the extra time to continue the conversation, but be prepared to respond to the child as soon as he requests your attention.

5. It helps if the child can literally *see* the conversation. If two adults hold a sleeve of the same sweatshirt, a corner of the same washcloth, or the opposite ends of a single piece of string, the child can see that he is not a participant in the conversation. If interrupted, refrain from talking to the child at all (saying anything to the child reinforces his interrupting behavior because he has managed to garner your attention). Instead, maintain eye contact with the other adult, and just point to the object which connects the two of you, and continue your conversation. If another interruption occurs, remove the child from the room without eye contact or comment, and return to your conversation.

Children, and too many adults, define *fair* as *same*. Giving each of your children a candy bar for a snack is the same, but if one of the children is diabetic, it is in no way fair. What is fair is giving each child a snack that each will enjoy.

Having the same bedtime for their children may make the parent's lives easier, but the children, who may be acutely aware of the age difference, may well resent this. It is a good idea to be sure that there is some recognition in daily family life that age differences result in differences in both *perks* and responsibilities. For instance, parents can explain, "Rene is old enough to have the *responsibility* of putting all of her toys away where they belong before bedtime, by herself. She also has the *perk* of being allowed to keep her light on to look at books for fifteen minutes after we say goodnight to her."

Taking such steps provides concrete recognition that *fair* means doing the right thing for both children, in the light of real differences between them.

## Activities

Adults get caught up in wanting the child's product to look nice to their adult eyes. For development of self-esteem, focus on providing opportunities for the child to access and develop his or her creativity and accept what looks nice, or is satisfying, to the child.

**Activity:** Cover a small table with a blanket. The child enters one end of the table as a small monster (seed, baby) and emerges from the other side as a fully grown, powerful monster (tree, adult).

Activity: Create a "Dress-Up" box that allows the child to try on/wear different roles (baby, policeman, father, super hero).

Activity: Grow plants from seeds (flowers for long-term projects and wheat grass or other sprouts for shorter projects). Seeds may be easily started in a cup which contains wet cotton balls or a bit of potting soil and water.

Activity: Have the child add and combine ingredients in a recipe for food, which is then cooked or otherwise prepared and consumed by the child. For example, fruit-flavored gelatin, baked goods, popsicles, salads, or pumpkin pie made from a whole pumpkin. Pretzels and gingerbread cookies are other sources of edible fun. These can be sculpted and possibly decorated before consumption.

Recipe for Pretzel Dough
Dissolve 1 Tbs yeast in 1/2 cup warm water. Add 1 tsp honey and 1 tsp salt. Add 1 1/3 cup flour and knead mixture. Roll pieces into shapes, brush with beaten egg, and sprinkle with kosher salt. Preheat oven and bake for 10 minutes at 425 degrees.

Recipe for Gingerbread Cookies
Heat 1 cup molasses to a boiling point. Add 1/2 cup sugar, 1/6 cup butter, 2 Tbs of milk, 4 cups flour. Add 1 tsp each: salt, baking soda, nutmeg, cinnamon, powdered ginger, powdered cloves. Form dough into balls the size the child can hold easily in his hand, and refrigerate the dough overnight. The next day the "dough-clay" can be played with, and eventually formed into shapes. The shapes can be decorated with raisins or currants, chocolate chips, nuts, candied cinnamon hearts, etc. Bake cookies at 375 degrees for about 10 minutes.

Corn Starch Stuff (to play with, not to eat)
Mix 1 part water, 3 parts cornstarch. Help the child mix and experiment with a little bit of cornstarch *clay*. Held in the hand it melts into a puddle. However, it can be rolled into a ball which maintains its shape for a few seconds before melting.

More Mixing Experiences
Make something requiring melting butter and chocolate, because the two substances easily combine into one liquid. By contrast, make salad dressing with spices, vinegar, water, and oil. When shaken vigorously, it may appear to the child that the three have combined. However,

the ingredients will soon settle into a colloidal suspension, with three distinct and separate layers.

Activity: Act out old-fashioned fairy tales such as "The Gingerbread Man" or "The Three Pigs" as you tell the story out loud together. If you do this with several children, it is important to give everyone the opportunity to experience all of the roles. At the end of the story, sit down together and ask the child what his favorite and least favorite part and character of the story is, and why. This can be done with children of different ages in the same group.

The child needs opportunities to sense and respond appropriately to both his own feelings and to the feelings of others. Opportunities to play at being the parent taking care of a baby—or the doctor who cures his patient—as well as playing at being the baby or the patient, provide important preparation for actual roles the child will encounter, or occupy, in his adult life. Playing at being a super hero provides opportunity to enjoy imagining having substantially more power and influence than he has in his daily life.

Hand puppets are fun and can be informative. The child may be more receptive to directions given by a puppet than to those given by the parent directly. Questions asked by the puppet on an adult's hand will often elicit more honest answers and more information from a puppet on the child's hand than an adult can get from asking the child directly. A five-year-old's sense of dignity may prevent him from answering an adult's questions directly. By contrast, his puppet may answer the query quite enthusiastically. For example, "Was the bear *very* sad when he had to stay with a baby sitter this morning, or only a *little bit* sad?"

When traveling, finger puppets can be a great time passer. This is particularly true if they are only available when traveling. Finger puppets can also be quickly made by making faces on the child's fingers with a magic marker.

The Blob (introduced in earlier chapters) can be used for fantasy play. With a dash of imagination it becomes a ship, an island, or a planet uninhabited by parents. It can also be used to practice the sequences required to accomplish any task: preparation, execution from start to completion, and recuperation and preparation for the next activity.

The child stands at some distance from the Blob. The parent alone, or with the child says, "Get ready, get set, go!" At the word "go" the child runs and jumps onto the Blob. The developmental progress for the child is to be able to refrain from moving until the word "go" is spoken. This helps prepare the child for school and other adult-organized activities where the child will be required to wait until instructions and the okay to start have been given before diving into the activity.

An "Inventor's Box" is the antidote to electronic devices. It is invaluable. It encourages creativity and advances small muscle ability. Unlike the two dimensional creative activities that electronic devices purport to provide, the Inventor's Box requires three-dimensional effort. In addition, all decisions concerning what to do, and how to proceed, are entirely up to the child. Therefore, he garners all of the self-esteem from the project. This is comparable to the difference between having the child apply crayons in a coloring book versus creating his own drawing from scratch.

Having children decorate already cut-out paper forms (for example, a leaf, a turkey, or a snowman) flies in the opposite direction from creativity. Let each child make his own version of these things.

Refer the child to the Inventor's Box whenever boredom is announced. Get in the habit of collecting things you would ordinarily throw away or recycle, such as:

- pull tabs from frozen juice containers
- cotton from newly opened vitamin bottles
- empty plastic medicine bottles/containers and their tops
- little boxes that new cell phones, jewelry, or checks come in
- ribbon and wrapping paper
- construction paper
- styrofoam packing peanuts
- lids from jars and canned foods (make sure edges are smooth)
- bottle caps from soda and beer bottles
- cardboard tubes from rolls of paper towels and toilet paper
- fancy chocolate boxes and *pillows* inside them that separate layers of candies
- small paper muffin pan liners
- duct, masking, and scotch tape, as well as glue, scissors, and magic markers

Give the child a cardboard box/carton and let him see how quickly he can rip it up into pieces small enough to throw into a small trash can.

If available, get partial rolls of unused newsprint paper from the company that prints your local newspaper, or get rolls of inexpensive, newsprint paper from an office supply store. This allows for large pictures or murals to be drawn. The child can lie down on the paper and have the outline of his whole body traced. The outline can then be filled in with markers or tempera paints.

If possible, have an easel with a tray at the bottom of it which securely holds containers of tempera paint. Use large pieces of newsprint paper and brushes with floppy bristles. This encourages a myriad of skills, from small motor control to learning about color combination, to spatial planning and well beyond.

Be creative with balloons. Inflate and tie the balloon. The object of the activity is for the child to keep the balloon from touching the ground for as long as possible, by tapping it with his hands. The child must keep both feet on the ground. Have older children try to take turns tapping or batting the balloon with their hands to keep it afloat, perhaps naming one item in a chosen category of things with each tap—for example, naming a different mammal, a kind of fruit, names of holidays, professional athletes, girls' names, boys' names, etc. with each tap

Have the child try to pop an inflated balloon with his bare hands (no fair using an object like a pin or tack). This is much harder than you might think. The more inflated the balloon, the easier it will be to pop. Many children fear that popping the balloon will hurt them in some way, and are quite reluctant to even try to do this. A surprising number of adults are similarly reluctant to try to do this.

See how many times a balloon can be batted gently between the hands of two children standing a short distance from one another, before it touches the ground.

Play with ping pong balls—have children stand all around a table, with their hands held behind their backs and their mouths at table level. Place a ping pong ball in middle of table, and give a signal for the children to begin blowing at the ping pong ball. For younger children, the goal is to see how long the ball can be kept from falling off an edge of the table. For children seven years or older, the children can form teams on opposite sides, competing to score points when the ping pong ball goes off the opposition's side of the table

See how long two children can hold a ping pong ball between their two foreheads. Teams of two children can compete if the children are at least seven or eight years of age. See which team can walk the farthest or the longest with the ping pong ball still in place.

Collages can be made by glueing different kinds of dried beans along with varying sizes and shapes of macaroni onto sturdy paper plates, trays or take-out food containers. Dried macaroni can be dyed in water tinted by assorted hues of food coloring. Allow the macaroni to dry, and then glue the pieces to a piece of cardboard or paper. Leaves, small stones, seed pods, and sticks collected from the yard or during a walk can also be used for collages.

Have the child place leaves she has collected between two sheets of waxed paper. Set an iron on the lowest possible heat and run the warm iron over the waxed paper. When cooled, the edges of the paper can be trimmed, and the creation hung in a window.

Small, interlocking plastic building blocks and pieces are good for untold hours of invention. If possible, have a wide variety of such pieces, not just pieces designed for construction of a single themed object. The child should be encouraged to combine even the pieces from themed project sets in ever changing ways.

Get a blunt sewing needle (plastic or metal) with a large eye, and thread it with yarn. Let the child sew shapes onto styrofoam trays.

Make a tent indoors out of a large sheet. Drape it over a table, or two chairs, or anchor three corners or sides and keep it puffed up by directing a stream of air from a fan into the tent.

Put four or five different kinds of small objects together in one container (for instance, buttons, stones, paper clips, rubber bands, feathers, cotton balls). Ask the child to sort them by type into separate containers. Older children can be asked to sort the family's clean clothing as it comes out of the dryer, into one pile of clothing for each family member.

Cook thick spaghetti until it bends (but isn't totally floppy). Drain in a strainer, rinse, and let spaghetti cool. Put a little glue into three or four small dishes. Mix different hues of food coloring into each dish of glue. Drag individual strands of spaghetti through the glue, removing excess glue by gently slipping each strand through thumb and index finger. Place them on waxed paper, forming sculptures. When dry these can be hung from light fixtures, or placed against windows, for viewing.

Construct a doll or toy animal house out of cardboard boxes. Make furniture out of small blocks, or smaller boxes. A sock placed over a block or two can make a bed; a handkerchief can be a blanket. Chairs can be made by attaching two paper cups together with a brad, bottom to bottom, and cutting a curved section out of the top cup to form the back and armrests of the chair.

Have the child help you measure out, combine, and mix different play doughs. Color each with different food colorings. Have the child sculpt with the different doughs and talk about any differences he observes in the properties of the doughs.

Play Dough #1
1 cup flour, 1 cup water, 2 tsp cream of tartar, 1/2 cup salt, 1 tsp cooking oil

Play Dough #2
1 cup flour, 1 cup boiling water, 1/2 cup salt, 1/2 Tbs powdered alum, 1 Tbs baby oil

Play Dough #3
1 cup flour, 2 1/2 cup salt, 3/4 Tbs cream of tartar

Mix in bowls and add just over 3/4 cup water and 1/2 Tbs cooking oil. Stir until all lumps are gone Add food coloring as desired. Pour into Teflon coated electric skillet, and cook over medium heat until the mixture balls up on your spoon. Remove from skillet. When it is cool enough to handle without discomfort, knead until cool. Oil your hands before kneading the mixture.

## Eight Activities for Birthday Parties:

1. Put twelve small pieces of candy, bite-sized crackers, or pretzels on a large plate. One child leaves the room and the group then decides which color or shape or type of snack is IT. The absent child then returns to the room and tries to guess which treat was chosen by the group, and gets to eat each wrong guess.

2. Have each child in a group construct a building with tiny marshmallows and toothpicks. Each child then describes what he or she notices about his or her building. Only the builder can speak about his or her construction.

3. Construct a "changing tunnel" out of large boxes duct-taped together, that the children can crawl through. Cut out windows in various places along the way. The children enter and travel through the tunnel one at a time. Before entering the tunnel, each child announces what type of creature he or she is now, and, after exiting the tunnel, into what he or she has changed.

4. An adult dispenses a dab of shaving cream onto one index finger of each of the children, asking them to see what they can *find, with emphasis on the child's imagination* (not what they can make, *which would emphasize the quality of the end product*). Have the children

verbally share what has been found, then erase what was found by rubbing their index fingers together until the shaving cream disappears. Then dispense more shaving cream and ask what else they can find. If the shaving cream is staying on their fingers up to this point, consider letting the children see what they can find using both hands, with the help of a bit more shaving cream. The only thing to outlaw is clapping their hands together, which will disperse the shaving cream all about (it will dissipate without ill effect).

If a child is having difficulty keeping the shaving cream on his hands, scrape the shaving cream off that child's hands, *without comment*, with your own hands. You will most probably find this child is suddenly quite willing to go along with the rules if given another chance. Plain shaving cream will not leave a stain; it is a clean mess. At the end of the activity, use your hands to scrape all of the cream that you can from the hands of each child. Tell the children that it is magic "clay" and that they can remove the remaining cream by rubbing their hands together until it disappears.

5. The children are seated close together on the floor in one room. There should be a bit of space around each child. The children are told to close their eyes. The adult then silently removes one child to another room, whispering an explanation of what is going on and what will happen next to the child being removed. Then the adult returns to the room where the rest of the children are waiting. The adult tells them to open their eyes and try to identify which child is missing. When they have correctly done this, the group can be asked to identify what colors or items of clothing the missing child is wearing. The missing child then returns to the group and the accuracy of the group's guesses is ascertained. Then all eyes are again closed, and another child is removed.

6. For children second grade and older: line up pieces of typewriter or construction paper in a row along one wall of a room. Leave about twelve inches between the pieces of paper. Have each child stand on one of the pieces of paper. There should be one more piece of paper than the number of children. Tell the children that no talking is allowed, and that the task is to get everyone across to the other side of the room in a line, without anyone touching the floor at any time.

Eventually they figure out the trick is to pass the extra piece of paper at one end of the line, to someone near the middle of the line, place it down on the floor in front of that child, and then have that child step onto it. That frees up a piece of paper at one end of the line. That paper can now be passed down the line and given to the child now standing one paper's length in front of the middle of the line. This child receives the paper, places it on the floor directly in front of him, and steps on it. The line now extends from the original middle of the line, two paper lengths in the direction of the opposite wall. This pattern is continued until the original line is replicated on the opposite side of the room.

7. Have children identify an object by feel, by placing the object in a box with a hole just big enough for the child's hand to pass through it. For younger children, use one object in one box. The children can either keep their guesses to themselves, or whisper them to the adult in charge. After everyone has had a turn, the box is opened, *without comment about the correctness or incorrectness of any guess,* and its contents revealed.

8. For older children, several objects can be placed in each of two baskets in advance of the activity, out of sight of the other children. A cloth is placed over the top of each basket. Have the children stand in a circle and count themselves off by saying, "one, two, one, two …" around the circle to determine two teams. Place the teams at a distance which prevents one team from hearing the conversation of the other team. Each team is given one of the covered baskets, and a pad and pencil. Each team member takes a turn putting one hand under the cloth, trying to identify the objects in the basket by feel. When each team member has had a turn, the team confers, and comes up with their team identifications for the objects, which are recorded on their pad of paper. Everyone is then brought together and the contents of the baskets are revealed. The team with the most correct identifications wins. Each team is awarded a small (different for each team) edible prize for playing.

## Self-Image – If All Goes Well Enough

If things go well enough during this stage, the child can use available physical space appropriately, respect boundaries between himself and others, assert himself physically, emotionally, and intellectually in appropriate ways, and lead, follow, and cooperate empathically.

Ideally, the ability to use energy to think, feel, and take action is sufficiently developed to support the child's belief that his capabilities and efforts, combined with the help of others, will allow him, like the protagonist in an old fashioned fairy tale, to succeed at given tasks enough of the time. His skills include:

When upset about an action he took, he feels guilt (a combination of sadness and anger about the particular action she took) and a desire to make a different behavioral choice in the future. He does not feel shame (i.e. that he is a bad person).

He has an internalized sense of right and wrong, of law and order.

His gender identity is set.

He can experiment and imaginatively play, trying out creative and diverse roles in society and the world.

Decisions about how and when to act on his thoughts and feelings are increasingly made in the light of intellectual and emotional information taken in and realistically evaluated.

He is increasingly interested in acquiring skills and in learning about family members, other families, and the world. For example, Nancy, Laurie, and I were about six years old. I remember not understanding why Nancy was so focused on spending time at Laurie's home, whenever Laurie's father was around. Several years later, Nancy explained that Laurie had told her that she (Laurie) knew who the tooth fairy was. It was her (Laurie's) father. Nancy had tried to spend as much time as possible at Laurie's house because she was hoping to catch sight of Laurie's father when he was being the tooth fairy, dressed in his tutu and tights!

The child's attention span increases during this stage, but it can still be difficult to interest the child in an activity which is not his choice at the time. The end of this period is marked by willingness to attend to an activity chosen by another, a strong indicator of readiness for kindergarten.

If all goes well enough during this stage, the child's self-perception, might be something like this:

"Since I have been given enough of what I need and want, the line between reality and fantasy is more reliably set. I am comfortable putting myself on the reality side when I need to. I see others as thought and feeling-filled people like myself. I can identify with my parents. I use my creative endeavors as effective ways of coping with my highly intense feelings. Since I can intuitively sense my own feelings and needs, as well as those of others, I can work both on my own, and with others, on a joint task with true empathic cooperation, at a leisurely pace, or with a sense of urgency, depending on the amount of time available."

The child completes activities and projects and is not overly concerned with the judgment of others about what he has done. He still cannot completely separate his sense of self from particular actions he takes. He can rebound from negative reactions he receives because he senses there will be time and opportunities in the future to try again to improve.

He can express and communicate his darker feelings, but doesn't have to do it immediately, or with the exact intensity and direction that initially occurred to him. For example, he can complain to his mother or father about his sister, or make up a play with his friends about a family with no sister in it. He can also express his feelings through creative activities like drawing, sculpting, dictating stories, or hammering nails into wood.

## Difficulties Linked to This Stage That May Emerge Later

The individual may have difficulty balancing his or her own needs and wishes, the needs of others, and constraints of the particular situation. She may be challenged starting a task and sustaining sufficient effort throughout a task, and/or completing a task. She may be unable to experience true empathy for another's position or situation—insisting, for instance, that her friend sympathize with her problem hangnail, when the friend just lost a job.

She may have difficulty achieving a balance in her conscience between over zealousness, and not being active enough. She may struggle with efficiently organizing space, time, and materials. Her creativity may be limited in activities, ideas, play, work, and/or problem solving. She may find it hard to respond to the particular person who occupies a particular role at a certain time, focusing rather on the role itself. For example, following an unsafe action advocated by the group's leader simply because it emanated from the group's leader.

# Latency: Six Years of Age to Puberty
## Chapter 6

### Use of Energy

Less effort needs now to be directed at managing his own self—so he can use his energy to acquire information and skills needed for understanding and learning about the world, for adequate functioning in school, for relationships with family, peers and their families, and to participate in group activities led by a variety of adults.

He can act with efficient cycles of exertion and recuperation of his physical, intellectual, and emotional effort. He can govern his energy outpourings based on the reaction they receive from his family and the wider world. He generally uses his energy in ways that will increase his overall competency.

### Thinking, Paying Attention, and Learning

Attention: First, he must choose the appropriate stimuli on which to focus. He must also choose which stimuli to disregard, whether arising from within the child (for example, an overriding emotional need to obtain and keep an adult's attention) or present in the external situation (for example, other visual, auditory or kinesthetic stimuli present while a teacher is talking).

At times, a single focus is appropriate (what he will write about his favorite holiday). At other times, he must simultaneously focus on multi-foci (both his own, and the ideas of others in the group writing project). Ability to appropriately single and multi-focus, and to shift between the two, increases during this stage.

Second, the child has to maintain attention long enough for information to be adequately absorbed. In addition, he needs to balance his need for attention from others with the attention he needs to expend on others, and simultaneously, on the work to be done in the present situation.

Third, paying attention requires recognition of the boundary between the child's self and other people—in physical space (refraining from poking an annoying classmate), emotional space (being comfortable when the teacher attends to another child), and temporal space (not interrupting a conversation in which he is not a participant).

Thinking and Learning: Prior to this stage, a substantial percentage of the child's thinking and learning has occurred through physical activity. He literally has been thinking and learning in action. During this stage, paying attention adequately to absorb information is followed by attributing meaning to that information through performance of operations that take place just in the child's mind (thinking). After this thinking has rendered the information meaningful, it is stored in the child's mind for later mental perusal, and/or for application in further mental operations, and/or in the child's chosen actions. In other words, it is learned.

Changes in thinking that occur during this stage include ability to:
1. Distinguish between mental and physical reality (social norms and physical events have different causes).

2. Intermittently understand multiple points of view (I want to stay up, but I also understand that my parents want time to themselves in the evening) and to change the way he views events and other people's situations (I thought my friend didn't like me, but I see now that he really does like me).

3. Understand that things existed before his parents existed (some volcanos were extinct long before there were people).

4. Think about what people do, how they do it, and about what causes events in the wider world (clouds come from evaporated water).

5. To realistically assess his ability to accomplish tasks in different situations, and perceive the cause and effect of his actions on others and in situations in the world (if I get ready for bed quickly, maybe there will be time for two bedtime stories).

As the child acquires knowledge about the rules of social interaction, his thinking changes in a known sequence. First he infers that the thinking of others is similar to his own way of thinking. Next, he recognizes that others can have thoughts different than his own thoughts. Finally, when he acquires abstract thinking, he can think about his own thoughts, enabling him to think about what another is thinking, and he understands that his own thoughts may be the subject of someone else's thinking.

Piaget called this stage the period of concrete operations, during which the child makes connections and performs mental tasks necessary for

realistic, logical perception of the physical world. Among these skills are the ability to:
1. Make logical inferences (conservation of volume and weight).
2. Think about the world in words, using spoken language to form a hypotheses (how many cookies will his grandmother let him eat for a snack?), after which he tries to identify general rules that explain the results of his experimentation (grandmothers are different than parents).
3. Use the knowledge he gains about rules, procedures, and expectations to adjust his behavior to meet the requirements of different situations (home, school, athletic team).
4. Break a concept into parts and see the relationship between those parts, and then combine parts into a single, whole concept.
5. Evaluate situations and information according to standard criteria. This allows him to monitor his own thinking and announce when he is ready to be tested on information he has learned.
6. Talk about hypothetical and future events (what would life on Mars be like or what he might want to do when he grows up).
7. Compare past and present events, and make good guesses about what caused the current situation, and what is likely to occur about that situation in the future (I can skateboard now better than I could last summer, and if I keep practicing, I bet I'll be really good at it by next summer.).

At the start of this stage he does not distinguish between an accident and an intentional act. If his model plane is crushed by his younger brother he believes that it was done on purpose, regardless of what his parents say to the contrary. By the end of the stage he recognizes that rules are created and agreed upon by individuals, and rules can be changed as necessary. He recognizes that morality depends on the individual's intentions, not just on the consequences of an action. The child who hangs a "Do not enter" sign on his door is experimenting with this concept.

Now he can change his thinking, based on new information or experience. For example, by ten or eleven years of age he has moved through the four stages of understanding about money described by Hans Furth, from thinking that everyone has money and that the shopkeeper gives you money when you buy something (actually the change from the bills you give him) to a realistic understanding of profit.

He uses language to learn about the world. He thinks and stores information in words. When angry at his mother, he doesn't try to hit her. Instead, he announces, "I'm going to my room and I'm never going to talk to you anymore," since he has learned that a verbal expression of his anger will have a more salutary outcome for him than the one used when he was younger.

Differences between similar objects can be quantified or measured. After being bitten by a dog, a younger child may change from thinking all dogs are friendly to thinking that all dogs are dangerous. By contrast, the child who is bitten by a dog during this stage learns that only some dogs are dangerous.

The child can memorize information. His ability to recall information increases measurably. His increasing ability to organize items by common features lead to his great interest in making collections.

The child sees himself as the one with primary responsibility for his learning, and he establishes a preferred thinking and learning style: observation, memory, trial and error, steps and sequencing, context, logic and reason, intuition, use of analogy, metaphor and imagery, or use of fantasy. He prefers to take in information aurally, visually, or kinesthetically. The teacher who refuses to let a kinesthetic learner fidget with his eraser (assuming he is not bothering anyone else) while the teacher is presenting material is in fact impeding this student's ability to absorb what the teacher is saying.

He is learning to accept, and respond effectively, to work that is both rote and new, easy and challenging, chosen by the child, assigned by teachers, or that has been decided on cooperatively.

There are dramatic increases in the child's fund of general knowledge and ability to analyze and respond to factual information and to integrate old with new information. There are also dramatic increases in the range and intensity of interest in intellectual challenges and exploration, including working with different media. He has preferences for areas of intellectual inquiry depending on his knowledge, experience, and skill.

## Sensing and Feelings: Assessing Responsibility

By the start of this stage, the child has easy access to the full range of feelings and good ability and willingness to identify and acknowledge what she is feeling and to link her feelings with real events (rather than to an imagined perception of what is happening). She can express her feelings in acceptable actions and, as she moves through the elementary school grades, she can increasingly do so in spoken language and writing.

The child is generally in a good mood and tends to be optimistic. She feels happy and her self-esteem increases as the result of her demonstrated ability in activities of all kinds—for example, completing lessons and assigned tasks on her own, expressing herself and communicating with a widening range of people, helping others.

Her ability to make increasingly realistic appraisals of herself, others, relationships, and events in the world increases. In turn, this increases her capacity for intimacy and tolerance for people who think and feel differently than she herself is feeling. She doesn't believe one person has to be wrong and the other right; she has room for different viewpoints. If her position is not accepted, she doesn't think "it's not fair."

Good reality testing also allows her to be healthily assertive in her dealings with others, rather than acting and reacting in passive or aggressive ways.

Although not always pleased to have to do so, she is willing to shoulder increasing personal responsibility as she moves through this stage, without feeling angry that she is being asked or required to do so. This is linked to her more realistic understanding that relationships involve reciprocal responsibilities.

It is normal for the child to be daily beset with the panoply of universally experienced fears: loss of parental love, bodily harm, death, illness, injury, punishment, loss of respect, and loss of self-esteem. However, these fears generally come up in connection with specific situations and, on her own or with a bit of assistance, she can adequately address them and they will dissipate rather quickly.

There are potentially enormous consequences if the child must daily confront realistically frightening or disturbing situations at home, as she travels about outside the home, or at school. All possible ways to lessen these occurrences should be taken, in the interest of keeping the child as safe as possible. There should be ongoing discussion between the child and her parents about the emotional impact this is having on both generations.

Negative emotional interaction between parent and child can be decreased, and in some cases avoided, if the parent responds to the feeling state that seems to underlie the child's statement, question, or behavior. For instance, child to parent, "Why do I have to take care of the baby this Saturday afternoon?" Parental response, "You sound pretty angry about having to take care of the baby, what's going on?"

The child may still have to babysit on Saturday afternoon, but discovering what was so onerous about this assigned responsibility, and addressing it, may lead to a better Saturday afternoon for all involved.

## Making Decisions and Taking Action

The child is interested in pursuing competence in activities of his own choosing, and needs opportunities to do so. His large muscle ability increases substantially, leading to greater interest in athletic activities, and in *make-pretend* games.

Competitive sports are now possible. Small muscle ability also leaps ahead, increasing his interest in complex physical activities such as taking things apart and in using electronic devices. It is likely that his facility and expertise in the last far surpasses that of his parents and significantly older siblings.

He enjoys assembling collections of items he finds interesting. His ability to self-regulate and to follow rules and concentration skills are established. Games with rules, like Monopoly, which involve acquisition and use of power and the interplay of chance and skill are of great interest.

As the child moves through this stage, the number of settings in which she spends significant time increases dramatically—it might include: the homes of friends, peer cliques, athletic teams, school bands or clubs, 4-H or Boy or Girl Scouts, and religiously-centered activities.

Each setting has its own explicit values and conventions of social interaction, along with ways to handle infractions of those values and conventions. Both have to be sufficiently learned, and to some extent internalized, by the child if she is to function successfully in each setting.

A primary source of increasing self-esteem during this stage comes from the child's interest in gaining and enjoying competent membership in these settings.

Contact with adults other than the child's own parents is an important source of learning, and provides exposure to new role models with which he can identify. Banding together in cliques or activity-related groups, and observing group rules helps increase the child's social interactional skills, and prepares the child for the idea that he will be able to function out in the world someday without his parents.

His increasing capacity for intimacy causes peer relationships to increase in importance. Peer relationships provide essential opportunities to learn how to form and maintain friendships and to manage the obligations and privileges of friendship.

Lacking such opportunities, the child may make friendship approaches to other children his age when engaged in a group activity when the focus is on the activity, not on forming individual friendships. Such approaches are likely to be ignored or rebuffed.

He learns to make good short- and long-term decisions as his organizational skills in the management of work and play activities increases.

He is willing to take reasonable risks in new situations, or in learning new academic skills. After seven years of age, he tolerates *messing up* in such attempts, and can rebound emotionally from such experiences. He can now see that the action he took was a *mess-up* rather than perceiving that he, himself is a "mess-up."

He is generally industrious and tries to get recognition for producing things. He is interested in completing tasks. He is curious and motivated to learn about and make orderly sense out of what occurs in the world.

He can accurately assess and accept the relative power he possesses in situations.

## School

The child and school in general: There are a number of significant factors that can have a crucial effect on the child's school experience, and thus, quite possibly, on her lifelong self-esteem. The match between the school and the family's culture, values and living style, and the child's ability to perform academically, socially, and athletically rank high among these factors. So does whether or not the child puts energy into completing her own tasks, rather than focusing on the work of classmates or social interactions with them.

School can be a haven if home life is chaotic. On the flip side, there are teachers who have done irreparable harm to the self-esteem of some of their students. School may be inherently more difficult for boys because they mature later, seem to have more disabilities, and may be allowed more leeway to challenge adults than girls are given. On the other hand, teachers have continuing difficulty engaging girls in mathematics and science, despite efforts to close this gap.

While parents are aware of the importance of the relationship between child and teacher and child and peers, they may be unaware of the importance to their child of another feature of the school experience. Here are three letters, written by third graders to their respective desks, at the end of the school year.

"Dear desk, I'm sorry that I slammed your lid. I liked making my stain glass picture on you and if I did not have you I would not be able to have done all of that nice work I did. I like you a lot, little buddy. And I am sorry that I wrote on you and put a number line and a name tag on you. Love, Marissa. P.S. I'm sorry I hit and punched you."

"Dear Desk, I am sorry I put crayon on you and slammed you so many times and hit you and wrote on you. I will miss you a lot because I am going to a different school. I liked writing on you. The thing I don't like is when I slammed my fingers in you. Love, Zander"

"Dear Mr. Desk, I hope you have a nice summer. Maybe I will see you next year. I'm sorry for what I did to you. Please write back. Love, Jill"

## Readiness for School

There are a number of skills that the child ideally has before he starts first grade. If these skills are not yet established, consider holding off entry into first grade for a year. This is likely to result in a happier and more successful academic experience for the child. Obtain a professional evaluation to determine what, if any, steps need to be taken in preparation for the child's entry into first grade the following year.

Skills indicating readiness for entry into first grade include:
1. Being responsible for his personal care in and outside the home.
2. Having small motor coordination sufficient to allow him to write numbers, letters, and geometric forms.
3. Ability to focus on and remember several directions given visually or orally (this involves attention span and distractibility, memory, and information processing).
4. Being respectful in his social relationships with peers and adults.
5. Being able and willing to follow through on a task of someone else's choosing.
6. Expressing his thoughts and feelings in acceptable ways.
7. Seeking help from adults in acceptable ways when needed, primarily to aid greater comprehension and participation in the ongoing activity (not simply to obtain and maintain adult attention).

## Family Life

Family life in general: Most frequently, the child grows up in the context of family living where he experiences the ups and downs of human relationships on the most basic level. There are serious consequences for the child if family life is very dysfunctional, or if the geographical area in which the child's life is conducted is dangerous. Both factors decrease the child's potential to find a positive way to succeed in society later, outside the family.

The main job of parents is to work themselves out of a job as gracefully as possible, by helping the child assume ever increasing responsibilities for management of his own life. Allocating time for individual, family, and couple activities, even if time is limited, continues to be important.

It is important that parents ensure that the child has contact with peers in and outside the home, even if the child doesn't request these activities or seems only mildly interested.

However, there can be a tendency to over-enrich the child's life with too many activities, eliminating potential creative opportunities. Creativity is born of boredom, which usually comes from spending time during which nothing is planned. Child to parent, "I'm bored!" Parent to child, "Great, that's what comes just before you decide what you will do next!"

Setting Behavioral Limits: It is wise for parents to create and maintain a caring atmosphere of mutual support between family members. This involves having realistic behavioral expectations for all family members. With respect to children, excessive assertions of parental power should be avoided, and so should setting inadequate behavioral limits. If the parents themselves grew up with behavioral limits that were either too strict or too lenient, it may be especially difficult for them to design and maintain behavioral rules that occupy middle ground.

Maintaining a boundary between parent and child permits establishment of lines of authority and responsibility that are needed for effective and pleasurable family life. It is helpful to talk about the responsibilities and the *perks* that both generations get. Children are often not aware or appreciative of the extent of parental responsibilities, and may be quick to rail against parental *perks*.

The three family rules described in an earlier chapter can cover a myriad of individual infractions: These rules are: #1 – No hurting of feelings or bodies. #2 – Do not take/borrow another's belongings without prior permission. #3 – Do not leave one area before cleaning up materials that were used in that space.

Lack of agreement between the parents about who will enforce behavioral limits, and how and when the limits will be enforced, can lead to the child creating or adding to a problem between the parents. This should be avoided. As previously noted, all the child needs to know is which parent's rules are to be observed (if the parents have previously agreed to differences between their respective behavioral requirements for the child in a particular situation or occasion).

Responsibility for violating rules for the use of electronic devices, as well as for behavior, should be properly placed on the offender. For example, parent to child, "I didn't take the video games away from my child. A bad choice made by my daughter resulted in their temporary loss. Until I recover from being lied to by my daughter the video games won't be available. Hopefully my daughter will make a different decision in the future."

It is unfair to let loose a lengthy, angry tirade on a child when you are also putting a behavioral consequence on him or her. That is a type of emotional double jeopardy.

Daily scheduling: School mornings are often complex events with all family members moving rapidly about, trying to launch into their respective activities. Planning ahead is helpful. Before bedtime the night before, have the child put out his clothing for the next day and gather together his homework and whatever he will need to take to school with him in the next morning.

If a good morning hug or verbal announcement that it is time to get up isn't effective, set an alarm clock in the child's room, and set a specific time the child is to be at the table for breakfast. Some children do best on their own, others do better if a parent is available for pleasant conversation as the child prepares for the day. In the second case, the parent needs to have taken care of his or her own morning preparation before waking the child.

Rather than continually reminding the child to keep moving through dressing and morning personal care routines, consider reading a book to the child. Simply stop reading when the child's forward progress stops. No parental comment is needed. Resume reading only when the child resumes his job.

Another technique is to give the child either a picture or a written list of things on the child's morning routine. Then, instead of reminding the child of what needs to be attended to next, refer the child to his list.

Leave the last ten minutes before departure for school to address any last minute needs in a pleasant tone. Instead of expressing anger at whatever didn't go well, compliment the child on what did go well.

Having a pleasant morning sets the child up for having a good day at school. It is usually clear to teachers whether the student has had a pleasant morning at home or not. The following letter highlights the emotionally important and direct linkage between the morning experienced by the child prior to arriving at school, and his school day. Ben was sent to the principal's office by his teacher who was concerned about the frequency of Ben's *put downs* of his classmates.

The principal asked Ben if he had an idea about why he had recently called a classmate "dumb looking." Here is Ben's reply, verbatim: "I've been having a bad day because my mom has been mad at me for a long time. It makes me feel bad and I let it out on other people. I try not to but it just comes out. I'm afraid to tell mom the truth when I do something bad because I'm afraid she'll be too mad at me, and then, when I tell the truth, she gets really mad! She's been mad at me for three days. I'm not afraid of my mom and dad divorcing, but my dad has high blood pressure, and gives me, or whoever comes downstairs, a hard time and gets all nervous and mad just like me. My mom comes to defend one of us, and she gets into it with Dad. Then he gets into it with her, and it turns into a whole family fight over tying shoes, or being late, or some stupid thing like that, and it makes me feel very sad."

"How can we help you here at school?" the principal asked.

"If I have a good day in the morning there, I'm okay here. If I have a bad morning at home, I don't have a good day here. I'll keep trying not to put kids down."

Fortunately, the principal at Ben's school kept a Blob in her office. She told Ben, "The Blob will be right here, and you can be excused to let some of your upset out on it when you need to, to help you not use put downs."

Homework: The child's homework is a contract between the child and the school. The parent should be a resource to the child but certainly should not do the homework for the child. That would prevent the school from knowing what the child in fact has mastered and in what areas he needs more help. It sends a message to the child that the parents believe the child isn't competent to do the assigned work.

If the child requests parental help, and is pleasant to the parent during the offered help, the parent should stay and help the child. Restrict the help you offer to the help requested by the child. The parent can feel free to point out that the parent does more for the child than the child's teacher and therefore won't accept worse treatment from the child than the treatment received by the child's teacher.

If the child cannot do the assigned work for whatever reason, offer to write a note for the child to take to school, stating that the child tried, but was unable to complete the work. The note should include what the parent expects from the teacher in response to the incomplete assignment—further clarification of the assignment, for instance, or perhaps some appropriate in-school consequence.

Some children need a quiet place to do their homework with few or no distractions. Other children can manage (evidenced by the grades they receive) their homework in the midst of family life.

Dinner time: Dinner times should not be a time for disciplinary discussions. If the parents model sharing how they felt about the best and the worst thing that happened during their own respective days, the child will be more willing to speak of his day.

Bedtime: Acknowledge the difference in the ages of the children in the family by having different bedtime routines, rules, and times. In addition, the parents need to acknowledge their right and desire to have time for themselves in the evenings, without the children.

Responsibilities the child has in family life: Before settling on responsibilities for the child, think back on your own experience. Were you given too much, reasonable, or too little responsibility? At what age did such work begin? Were the jobs inside the house or did you work outside the home? Were you expected to contribute your efforts to the household with monetary remuneration, or without it? What was the consequence of failing to carry out your assigned job? Discuss your respective experiences with your partner, and only then decide on what jobs to assign your children and at what ages the jobs should be assigned.

Work responsibilities should be clearly described to the child when his full attention is available. Giving such descriptions while the child's eye is on an electronic device is pointless. Once job assignment has been made, write a contract between the child and you, specifying what is to be done, to whose standards, and by when it is to be completed. Post the contract somewhere it is easily visible if it is a repeating job. It is often helpful to show the child what the completed job looks like.

Whether or not the child is told in advance what the consequence, if any, will be if completion of the assigned task is unsatisfactory depends on what will be most effective with the particular child involved. Give a child under nine years old a warning that it is almost time to begin the job and let him know when work time has arrived. Wait until at least nine years old before assigning the child responsibility for the regular care of an animal or for music or other lesson practice times.

A child nine years old or older is likely to feel anger at the parent for *trying to control him* unless given advance notice of work. However, once job parameters have been made clear, no reminders or comments about the job should be made until the deadline for job completion has been reached.

If the job is incomplete, the child should first know you are pleased about what was completed satisfactorily. Then let the child know (without a tirade of anger or disappointment) what needs to be done now to complete the job, or what needs to be done differently in the future. Any consequence imposed should befall only the child. Remember that visiting both an angry tirade and a consequence (for the same infraction or failure) is inappropriate.

Compliance for work assignments is usually improved if an older child has greater responsibilities along with more perks than the younger child.

Allowances: If the child receives an allowance, it should be in line with his ability to manage it. It should not be used to apply pressure for achievement or obedience, nor withheld in times of anger, nor used as a reward for good behavior. Any financial obligations that the allowance is to cover should be clearly stated, and the money given should include discretionary funds that the child can save or spend without parental comment or judgment.

## Changes That Occur Two Years Before Puberty

An indicator that puberty has not yet begun is evidenced in this child's reaction to being given an explanation of sexual intercourse: "You mean people do this for fun?"

Changes that harbinger the approach of puberty will be evident. A cognitive shift occurs as the child acquires abstract thinking ability. He can see new kinds of logical relationships. Neurological and endocrinological triggers cause an increased release of sexual hormones, a spurt in physical growth, and development of primary and secondary external sexual characteristics. Up to about fifteen years of age, girls mature faster than boys, both intellectually and physically, and this causes difficulties in the relationships between them. When boys are horrified at the changes in their own bodies, that are out of their control, abstract thinking helps them cope—for example, through increased fascination with monster and horror movies and video games.

Emotionally, there is increased competition between girls of this age. They also have markedly ambivalent feelings towards their mothers and tend to devalue them. Many mothers report that during either during their daughters' twelfth or thirteenth year, they experienced close relationships with their daughters, but by contrast, experienced conflicted relationships during the other year.

Boys are ambivalent about receiving nurturing from their mothers and devalue females in their fantasies. They talk to, and about, their mothers in disparaging ways—or even under their breath while being intentionally loud enough for their mothers to hear.

Boys and girls both tend to have one or two best friends during this period. Peer groups increase in importance because they share the same concerns and anxieties about the changes that are occurring. Therefore, talking with peers helps kids this age to manage their common anxieties—it is easier for them to talk with peers than with their own parents.

Both boys and girls tend to show an increased interest in bathroom jokes, and are sloppy in the care of their bodies, belongings, and bedrooms. There is an increase in modesty but there may also be intermittent exhibitionistic behavior.

Boys are increasingly self-centered. They like to talk with friends about girls but won't approach a girl directly. Masturbation fantasies increase. At times they act like much younger children.

## Situations That Should Be Addressed If They Occur During this Stage

### Over-Involvement With the Child

A parent may have enjoyed a close relationship with the child, but during this stage the child is increasingly involved in the world outside the home. The parent needs to become comfortable with this. In the three instances described next, the real reason for the over involvement had to be identified and acknowledged before the situation could change.

Albert's mother had not adjusted to increased separation between herself and her eight-year-old son. She was in the bleachers watching Albert compete in a swimming meet in the pool below. Her eyes were riveted on her son and every time Albert took a breath with an open mouth, she did likewise.

If the child correctly perceives that his parent cannot emotionally afford to *lose* her to school, the child may oblige by acquiring physical symptoms requiring her to stay at home—apparently too ill to go to school in the morning or to remain at school for the entire day. Mary's symptoms disappeared when she was permitted to remain at home with her mother.

When April's mother was a child, she had been molested in the mornings by the caretaker at her elementary school. When April was in third grade, her mother was still accompanying April into the classroom every morning, in spite of April's repeated and reasonable request that her mother go with April only as far as the playground, so April could enjoy playing with her friends before the start of school.

## Experience With Serious Illness and Death

Adults need to take the lead in initiating continuing open discussions about serious difficulties being experienced anywhere in the family, in order for children to believe it is permissible to express their feelings, ask questions, and ask for attention in acceptable ways. Here is an example of what happened in a family when it was initially thought that talking would make things worse.

The father suddenly became seriously ill. The mother and grandparents decided that it would be better not to talk about the illness. Soon, the eight-year-old's teachers notice a marked change in the child; she became aggressive and uncharacteristically un-talkative. The teacher and school counselor talked with the parents and grandparents about the situation. As a result, the family sought some professional support and began to talk openly about the sad situation. Almost immediately the child's behavior returned to normal.

At that point the six-year-old in the family, who up until this point had evidenced no marked upset over the father's illness or her sibling's changed behavior, began to have *meltdowns*. She had previously put expression of her own feelings on hold until there was permission to express and communicate her feelings and receive emotional support from her mother and grandparents.

Here is an example of how adults can offer an opportunity to a child to express her deep sadness: Marissa's third grade teacher asked each student to write a letter to his or her mother, as a Mother's Day present. The teacher reassured Marissa that she could write a letter also, if she wished, in spite of the fact that Marissa's mother had died the previous year. Here is Marissa's letter to her mother:

"Dear mom, I'm sorry about what happened and I miss you. I wish you could come back but you can't cause you're already dead. I am so sorry about what happened. I will always send you a letter. I'm so sorry. I wish you weren't dead. I wish none of our family were dead. I feel so sorry for you. And remember this. I really love you very much."

## Anxiety

The cause of excessive anxiety needs to be determined. For example, does a child's extreme anxiety whenever his parents go out for the evening stem from the child's interior, feeling life, a difficulty in the family, a traumatic event that the child has experienced? Or, is there some other cause?

## Learning Difficulties

Learning difficulties may have already been noted or may emerge as academic expectations increase in the early grades. How they are handled by the family and the school can have an enormous effect on the child's lifelong self-esteem. Three important steps need to be taken if such difficulties are suspected.

First, parents need to tell the child that they have noticed, or have been told, that he seems to be having an extra amount of difficulty completing his school work—that it is not fair that this is so—and that the parents are going to find out whether he needs some extra help. If he does, they will try to get it for him. The parents should point out that while schools have lots of testing for reading, writing, and math, there are no tests for other skills that are also very important, such as kindness, courage, curiosity, openness to new experiences, or musical and athletic ability.

Parents should share their own experiences, both positive and negative, if they themselves had learning difficulties. Fortunately, there are numerous books out on this subject that can be shared with the child to mitigate against his perception that he is the only child experiencing such difficulties.

Secondly, parents should take effective steps to see if there is, in fact, a learning difference, and if so, determine the particular area and extent of it. It is wise to consider starting with a physical examination with a pediatrician, to see whether apparent academic difficulties have a physical base, which may be easily corrected. For example, Tony's third grade teacher thought that he might have a vision problem. She decided to talk to Tony first. The teacher picked up two pencils, held them tightly together, and wrote his name in large letters on a piece of paper, trying to give Tony an example of double vision. She asked Tony if words ever looked the way she had just written his name.

Tony shook his head and said, "No." The teacher began to mentally prepare for a conference with the parents to suggest a visit to an ophthalmologist. However, before she could mentally organize her plan, Tony picked up three pencils, held them tightly together, wrote his name, and said, "But words look like this some of the time."

Gather and share with your pediatrician what the child reports about his school situation, what you have noticed at home, and information you gather from his teachers' perspectives.

Unfortunately, many parents have accepted the school's assessment that their child can do the work, but just isn't trying hard enough. The self-esteem of many a child with a learning difference has been severely damaged by the child repeatedly hearing teachers say, "You can do it, I know you can. You just need to try harder!"

A fourth grader who does not have dysgraphia may be able to write a good paragraph in ten minutes. A paragraph of equal quality can be written by a fourth grader with dysgraphia, but it may take that child an entire hour to do it. Two issues need to be considered. First, does the child have the innate ability to do the assigned work? Second, why is the child having to expend so much energy and time to complete assignments, when he appears to possesses adequate ability to do so.

Some public school districts are quite reluctant to acknowledge (evidence to the contrary) the presence of learning differences in their students. These schools may be legally responsible for the costs of proper testing to assess the student's situation and for the costs of providing supplementary educational services if the school acknowledges the need for these services. They may wish to avoid the expense of these services.

School is the child's workplace, and the longer that a learning difficulty negatively impacts the child's performance, the more damage is done to his or her self-esteem. It is very important, therefore, to get proper testing and needed help in place as soon as possible, and well before fourth grade, when academic demands measurably increase.

Some learning differences are relatively easy to address in the classroom. For example, Martha was able to demonstrate adequate comprehension of the material if she was given the extra time she needed to take written tests. Unfortunately, Martha's teacher defined fair as *same* and maintained that giving Martha extra time would be unfair to the other children in the class. In fact, what is fair is giving each student the opportunity to demonstrate capability, even if the time Martha requires to do this is greater than that needed by her classmates.

A child with a learning difficulty that is un-diagnosed and not addressed may become over concerned with *fairness* everywhere in his life. All a parent can do is to state what is true in the particular circumstance. For example, "I think it is quite unfair that you have a learning difficulty, but I do think it's fair that you take out the trash for your sister tonight, since she is ill and can't do her job."

In addition, the child may vehemently deny responsibility for any negative behavior of his, or he may get angry frequently without obvious cause, become disruptive in class, or become the class clown. He may withdraw, regress, stop trying in school, or seem depressed.

One type of learning difficulty has to do with paying attention. It is important for parents of a child with attention difficulties to remember that these may occur intermittently, feeding adult perception that the child could do better if he tried. A child with this difficulty, when reminded before dinner of a task to be done after dinner, is not necessarily going to remember to do it once dinner is over. If you remind him that he had been informed earlier of what he was to do, he is most likely to protest vehemently that "You never told me to do it!"

Keep in mind that this child is massively frustrated because he has this same difficulty following his teacher's instructions, and with taking in all of the academic information his teacher presents, and/or retrieving, using, or demonstrating possession of that information later when required to do so.

If the services of a tutor are sought, be sure, through your own research, that the tutor you select has received specialized training in helping children with learning differences. It is sometimes helpful to explain to the child that he needs a learning coach who helps children in the learning coach's area of expertise, just as athletic coaches do in their field.

Parents may avoid getting testing for their child, or extra academic help because they fear the consequences of the child being labeled. In fact, there is something worse than labeling. The child's lifelong self-esteem is at peril if needed help is not obtained.

Parents should emphasize that every person has difficulty in some area of his or her life. Some people are mean and some selfish. Some have difficulty balancing on skateboards or following diagrams for assembly of simple plastic vehicles. Some difficulties are visible, some are not. Some appear sooner and some later in life. Some people have physical difficulties that cannot be addressed. Tell your child what has been particularly difficult for you to do in your life. Look for opportunities to acknowledge skills that your child possesses and support him in gaining ability in some endeavor of his choosing in which he can be successful.

## Separation and Divorce

The parent must consider the child's developmental situation when telling him or her about an upcoming separation. Ideally, parents tell the child about this together, regardless of their own beliefs about which partner (if it's not a mutual decision) is the *cause* of the separation. It would be unfair on the face of it for this important event to be left in the hands of only one parent. In addition, having both parents present ensures that each knows exactly what the other parent has said to the child, and that the child has heard directly from each parent. Hopefully, this announcement occurs some time before the actual separation.

If possible, show the child where each parent will be living after the separation occurs. The child should be given opportunities to ask questions about the separation. It is essential to take the child's concerns and questions seriously. While the parents may be focused on their adult relationship, the child is concerned about how important, concrete events in her daily life will be affected by the separation. Where will she live after the separation? Who will feed her guinea pig? How will she get to and from school and after school activities? When will she see each parent? The child's underlying questions concern whether or not she will be taken care of in spite of the change in family life.

Until abstract thinking is acquired, the child believes herself to have in part caused the parental split. The parents must tell the child on repeated occasions, initiated by the parents, that because they think like grownups, they do not think it possible for children to cause their parents to separate.

Give the child concrete examples of the difficulties in the marriage that contributed to the separation. The young child cannot make any sense at all out of "We were incompatible," or "We just didn't get along," or "We disagreed too much." Think of ways these difficulties were visible to the child. For example, "I liked having dirty clothes put in the hamper but my partner thought it was all right to leave them on the floor." Or, "I liked staying home on the weekends, but my partner wanted to go out to parties and restaurants every weekend, all weekend."

This identifies differences between the parents without fixing blame. Outright blaming statements should be avoided, because an attack upon one parent by the other parent literally emotionally splits the child's loyalty in half, with neither half being found acceptable. It is therefore also important that each parent identify specific things they like and respect (or at least used to like and respect) about one another.

It is additionally the responsibility of the parents to repeatedly bring up the subject of how the changing situation is affecting everyone. It is entirely insufficient to tell the child once that "You can talk to me whenever you like about the separation." The child must be invited into such a conversation, with the parent beginning the conversation by speaking about at least one thing of emotional importance to the parent that the parent is experiencing due to the ongoing situation.

If at all possible, reach agreement over custody arrangements without court involvement. This allows maximum flexibility as circumstances change. Keep the focus of negotiation on the best way to meet the child's developmentally linked needs. Remember that libraries are excellent venues for discussions where there is concern that emotions may run high.

If the child is not going to have regular contact with both parents, or if there is particularly difficult communication between the child and one parent, it may be helpful to give the child a book in which to draw or write. In it, the child can record significant events, feelings, and thoughts at the time they occur, for one of two purposes: the book can be shared with the infrequently seen parent at a future date. Or, if it is for some reason unwise to share the book's contents with a particular parent, it can be kept in a safe place. Venting feelings in the book may diminish the likelihood of the child's feelings being expressed in unwanted behaviors. It speaks to the child's hope that circumstances in the future might permit the sharing of the book's contents.

Do not permit the child to play an active role in arranging negative contact between his parents. Separate a telephone conversation the child is having with one parent from a telephone conversation between the two parents needing to hash out some difficulty between the two of them. And neither parent should ask or demand that the child carry troubling messages between the parents, whether on the telephone or in person.

It is wise to keep any new partners of the parents as much out of the child's awareness as possible, unless the relationship has lasted at least six months and is expected to be ongoing.

Children almost always harbor the hope and/or belief that the parents will get back together, despite even overwhelming evidence to the contrary. While children are generally supportive to parents grieving over the demise of their marriage, they find numerous ways to express unhappiness at the parents' new important adult relationships. For example, five-year-old Jerry said the reason he didn't flush the toilet was in order to annoy his father's new girlfriend. Nine-year-old Betty said she looked sadder than she really felt, in order to inspire her mother to send away the mother's new partner.

## Remarriage

Remarriages in which there are children from each parent living in the new home are often referred to as "blended families." This is a complete misnomer. When melted, chocolate and butter do blend together. However, the ingredients of salad dressing (spices, oil, vinegar, and water) do not. They may look so when vigorously shaken. However, they soon settle out into three distinct layers. Salad dressing is a colloidal suspension. A remarriage when children are involved might be aptly termed a "colloidally suspended family."

Unfortunately, time is not often spent honoring the fact that the new marriage is a combination of parts of three separate families, and all three have enduring emotional importance to the children involved. Once living in a colloidally suspended family, children overwhelmingly report they rarely, if ever, have Special Time with their original parent, although they crave such time. Children have less difficulty with the way parents in the blended family organize family life if Special Time is regularly scheduled.

For the first six months, household rules decided upon by the parents should be enforced if at all possible by the child's original parent. The exception to this occurs when the child is told that the stepparent will be in charge for a particular situation or period of time.

Differences in the way family life is conducted in the two different homes in which the children may spend time should be acknowledged, but parents in each household should stand firm on the regulations they set in their respective *new* homes. In addition, one parent should not be asked to discipline a child for a problem that occurred in the other parent's home. The children should be given permission not to like the stepparent, although they should be required to treat the stepparent with respect. This, like the "Bad Baby Doll" (described in the section "Preparing for the Arrival of a New Baby") increases (although counterintuitively) the chances for a positive relationship between stepparent and children.

Other steps that may ease life in the new family include: giving the child some time and space to make the transition between different households before being required to actively join that family's activities; giving the child a calendar of his own on which important events are recorded in each household; advance notice of time he or she can count on spending in each parent's household; a specific schedule for Special Time with each parent from his original family.

Each *original* parent should take opportunities to hear in private how the new family arrangement is impacting the child, and should take effective steps to address the child's concerns. The parents should listen to concerns about specific behaviors and situations, but not, for example, to diatribes about the whole person the stepparent is.

It is important to directly confront a child for behavior that is annoyingly and strikingly similar to behavior previously exhibited by the absent parent. For example, "I thought it was inconsiderate of my former wife to leave her wet towel in the shower, and that was one reason we didn't stay together. I won't accept that behavior from my child in this household."

## Illness In a child

Illness in a child is always frightening to parents, especially when they must rely on the expertise of medical personnel. It is therefore important to find a medical doctor or team of health care providers you trust and with whom you communicate well. Parents need a clear understanding of the illness itself and its expected course with the child. If the illness is chronic, you need to know whether the condition is expected to be constant, relapsing, or episodic.

Get assistance from medical personnel and professionals knowledgeable about child development if you are not sure what information to present to the child, given the child's developmental stage. It is also helpful to get assistance in determining what should be shared with other family members.

At times, a child may seek to protect parents by not discussing aspects of his illness that are particularly frightening to him. If possible, find ways to involve the child in some aspect of the management of his illness. This fosters responsibility and self-esteem. If the child is old enough, consider having direct communication between the child and medical personnel.

Parents need to set aside time for themselves as individuals, as well as a couple, in order to share their concerns about the child who has the illness, the needs of other family members, and to nurture their relationship with each other.

Since a child's illness has a powerful (even if not outwardly visible) influence on all family members, it is often helpful to get professional support for the family. Among the issues that need to be addressed are: who is and is not involved in the child's care; practical and emotional effects of changes in the roles family members occupy, including possible over-involvement of the primary caretaker; and the child's upset over her increased dependence.

## Sexual Abuse

The very young child (under four years of age) believes that the parent knows whatever the child knows. For this reason, a young child may not tell the parent about the abuse. Unless the parents bring up the subject of possible abuse with the young child, the child may believe that it is talking about the abuse, not the abuse itself, which is unacceptable. It is wise, even with an older child, to ask the child who reports abuse whether or not the child believes the parent already knows about it.

The parent must express belief in the truth of what the child reports, and repeatedly reinforce that the child did nothing wrong, and that the parent is going to help the child. The first step in providing help is to ensure the child's safety. A report should be made to the appropriate authorities, and an investigation should be made. If abuse is determined to have occurred, law enforcement should respond appropriately. In addition, several more steps need to be taken by the family.

1. Professional help should be sought for the child as an individual and for the other family members, all of whom will have strong emotional responses (whether apparent or not) to what has happened.

2. It is essential to ascertain the meaning the child attributes to the abuse. For instance, the child may have gained self-esteem from having been *chosen* by the only person who, in the mind of the child, truly cares for the child.

## Depression and Sadness

Sadness occasioned, for example, by the loss of a loved one, usually doesn't last more than three months. Depression, on the other hand, generally lasts longer. Depression in children presents more often as anger than it does as sadness. This exacerbates the situation, because it is more difficult for parents to be supportive when the child misbehaves out of anger than when the child appears to be very sad.

The parent must seek professional help whenever any of the following occur: the child talks about wanting to hurt or kill himself or others; when his language or actions indicate a preoccupation with death; when enuresis (bedwetting) or encopresis (fecal incontinence) is present; when there is extreme aggression or sibling rivalry; when there is a total absence of sad feelings when sad feelings would be appropriate; or there are intense and persistent irrational fears.

In considering whether or not to seek professional help, it should be remembered that at times the child may be *carrying* the depression of another family member when that is not being effectively addressed.

## Self-Perception – If Things Go Well Enough

The child from six to puberty: His small and large muscle ability allow him good skill and control over the quantity and quality of his physical exertions. He can regulate withholdings and outpourings of his intellectual, emotional, and social energy so that the intentions of his actions most frequently have their desired impact.

He usually chooses the appropriate focus for his attention and sustains his focus long enough for adequate comprehension. He has reasonable memory of the past and he plans for the future. He believes in his ability to function academically and in his ability to absorb general principles and information about the world. He learns from observation, trial and error, mentors, and role models. He has learned a great deal about how events in the world occurred.

He realistically acknowledges and manages the full range of his positive and negative feelings. He can tolerate frustration and ambivalence in his thoughts and feelings, and the thoughts and feelings in others reasonably well. He realistically assesses the power he has in a situation, relative to that possessed by others, and acts with appropriate assertion rather than with aggression (which can be expressed as passivity or passive aggression).

He has gained a great deal of knowledge about how relationships are conducted and he honors the obligations and privileges of his friendships (fairness, loyalty). He has one or two really good friends and peer relationships are very important to him. He realistically compares the level of his performance in different endeavors to that of his peers.

He attends to and accomplishes tasks chosen by himself and by others. He can work on his own and with others, both in and out of home, and bases his actions on consideration of his own needs, the needs of others, and circumstances of the particular situation, such as given time limits for task completion.

He has found something that he is interested in pursuing, that he does well, and that gets him recognition from those important to him. He understands and accepts that he has to cope in the external world where criteria for judgment of his actions, work products, and behavior differs from his experience at home. He understands that recognition for his actions depends not on his intentions but on the results of those actions. He is reasonably optimistic about the outcome of his activities at home, in school, and in the wider world.

## Difficulties Linked to This Stage That May Emerge or Worsen Now and/or Later

If the child realistically assesses herself as significantly less capable than her peers in one or more areas of great importance to her, she feels some amount and intensity of anger and sadness. However, perceiving that she has primary responsibility for her own learning and performance, she will often initially increase her efforts in order to improve her own performance. She will sustain this increased effort for a time. If her performance continues to fail to match the performance level of her peers in spite of her efforts, her anger and sadness intensify, self-esteem will suffer, and she may stop trying so hard, or stop trying at all. Lacking abstract thinking ability until the end of this stage, she believes she is at least partly responsible for all that happens to her. She doesn't know what she has done, or is doing, to prevent her performance from improving. Damage to the child's self-esteem may be mitigated if her performance equals or exceeds that of her peers in other areas of her life that she deems important.

However, if the area of difficulty involves academic performance, or another area of extreme importance to the child (peer relationships, athletics) and the child does not receive proper diagnosis of her difficulty, support from her parents, and the help needed to make good enough progress, or if her difficulty cannot be remediated, let alone advanced, her self-esteem will very likely be significantly impacted.

In this situation a snowball effect often ensues. The child's upset at her inability to succeed leaks into her language ("math is dumb"), and her academic performance (school assignments aren't handed in), and into her behavior in other areas of her life (she protests that job assignments at home are grossly unfair to her).

It is unlikely that academic difficulty, that originates or becomes more important in this stage, will dissipate on its own. More often, the child's upset continues, spreads, and picks up momentum and mass, like a snowball rolling down a mountain, increasingly damaging her self-esteem as she moves through this stage, through adolescence and well into her adult life. It is crucial to effectively diagnose and tackle difficulties the child experiences during this stage as soon as possible.

Significant difficulties establishing satisfying peer relationships, not being a valued member of at least one group, and lack of at least one adult who cares about and mentors the child can all result in long lasting damage to a child's self-esteem unless adequately addressed during this stage. These circumstances negatively impact the individual's belief in her ability to lead a productive and satisfying life in society as an adult, and may well become a self-fulfilling prophecy.

## Activities

Many, if not most, activities described in the section covering ages three to six years of age can be easily made more challenging in order to be appropriate for children of latency age. In addition, the child's range of music pursuits, athletic endeavors, and group or club activities can be expanded as the child grows through latency and his or her particular interests are identified and pursued in the wider world.

# Adolescence
## Chapter 7

### Overall View of Adolescence

The word "adolescence" comes from the Latin word "adolescere," that means "to ripen" or "to grow up." It is the period of physical and psychological development that begins with the onset of puberty and the capacity for reproduction—ejaculation of sperm in males and menstruation and ovulation in females. In this country and others, there are no specific markers for the end of this stage. However, there is a general expectation that by the end of this period the individual is prepared and willing to assume a responsible place in the adult world of work and reciprocal, emotionally-significant relationships. In this writing the focus is on the years roughly spanning junior high school (twelve to fourteen years of age) through the end of high school (eighteen or nineteen years of age).

With the acquisition of abstract thinking, all previously held ideas the adolescent has had about himself, relationships, and the world must be reworked. The enormous physiological and emotional changes occurring in this stage prompt a reworking of all of the major issues of earlier stages of development. Change and growth occur in jumbled order and often at wildly fluctuating rates and intensity. For this reason, adolescence is frequently referred to as a time of "normal craziness."

The goal is for the adolescent to see himself as a worthwhile person with realistic hopes of achieving a satisfactory enough place in the adult world of work and relationships. The individual's trek through adolescence is easier if he has adequate ability in skill areas emphasized in the years prior to the onset of puberty.

To parents, one of the most annoying changes is the adolescent's ability to see clearly through the parents' faulty logic. Two of the most terrifying changes are the fact that the adolescent is no longer in the care of a responsible adult when he is not with a parent, and that he has access to some frightening action choices (alcohol, drugs, sexual activity, internet porn sites, and chat rooms). The adolescent may choose such actions during the very moments when his judgment and reality testing resemble that of a much younger child.

## The Stages of Adolescence

Adolescence falls roughly into three stages, each of which has somewhat different characteristics and goals.

### Early Adolescence
### (twelve to fourteen years of age)

Hormonal changes result in the adolescent's increased focus on his or her own body. Irritability and disagreements with parents, peers, and school life increase. As physiological changes occur, the adolescent experiences a roller coaster of fluctuating emotions. Intense emotional ties with parents are challenged by the need to establish his or her own identity and relationships with others outside the family.

The adolescent may try to keep her emotions in check by being reluctant to express much emotion at all with family members. Friendship and dating are sources of recreation, status, and ways to sort out and begin to establish her own identity, behavioral standards, and beliefs. These relationships are based on mutual interests and a desire to be popular in her peer group.

Relationships with one or two close friends provide opportunities to correct distortions about how to conduct successful, emotionally significant relationships. Dating and sexual experimentation is influenced by the values of the adolescent's parents, and the values espoused by social and religious authorities, media, and peers.

Some rebellion to parental rules is necessary for the adolescent to establish his or her own identity. For example: he wants to choose his own clothes and friends; his behavior is gross at times; curfews are strongly resisted. In a family with few rules, adolescents may try to impose their own rules on the family.

Mother-son relationships need to change from any *power over* basis to insistence on the mutual, empathic cooperation needed between any two people living together. This shift needs active backing of the boy's father. For example, "I won't let my wife be talked to in a disrespectful way."

An allowance should be given at less frequent intervals and be increasingly used by the adolescent to cover his or her financial responsibilities (cosmetics, the cost of recreational activities, clothing).

## Middle Adolescence
### (fifteen to seventeen years of age)

Sexual identity becomes fixed. Romantic love relationships in both fantasy and real life involve the adolescent seeing aspects of herself in her partner in order to see those parts reflected back to her, and to clarify what she likes and does not like in herself.

Adolescents don't recognize that they are conflicted between their desire to make their own decisions and shouldering the responsibility of doing so. The height of family turmoil is often reached during this period because the adolescent is at the height of her personal identity confusion. Adolescents are wildly unhelpful at home and wildly helpful in other situations, and this drives the parents crazy. Adolescents see their parents as caricatures of themselves and mock them as a way to sort out parts of themselves that are and are not like their parents.

By the end of this stage, their egocentrism decreases and their personalities begin to integrate. This allows humanization of adolescents' views of their parents, and they both accept and reject some aspects of them, and of themselves. In addition, adolescents become better at giving and taking in relationships with others in both fantasied and real life romantic love.

## Late Adolescence
### (eighteen to nineteen years of age)

His sexuality is now under more control. He is consolidating his identity as an individual, so less energy is tied up with his personal history. He feels more connected to the values of his family and social group. He begins to see himself more clearly, and empathy with others increases as his egocentrism dims. His interest in home and school is more realistic, and so are his plans for what he will pursue after high school. Some clashing emanates from both parents and adolescent because of their impending separation and the mixed emotions this occasions.

In the United States this period can extend well into the late twenties due to economic opportunities and circumstances, educational pursuits, and individual and family issues.

## Use of Physical Energy

The adolescent's use of physical energy fluctuates wildly. Differences appear between the sexes with respect to the amount of physical strength and the ways that it is used. Assessment of the effort required to accomplish a task (to keep a friendship, complete a homework assignment, to get somewhere on time) is often unrealistic. The adolescent's employer finds him energetic and efficient. However, at home he can't keep track of his own belongings. He lacks modulated changes between the physical effort he expends and recuperation from that exertion. He is far too exhausted to do household chores or spend a particular evening with family members. However, he can mobilize himself in thirty seconds to play eight hours of soccer with his buddies, if suddenly invited to do so. He is either in total motion or falls like a felled tree onto the couch, virtually inert for a period of time.

## Reworking of the Hallmark Skills of the First Stage of Development

During adolescence, reworking of the Hallmark Skills of the First Stages of Development occurs as a result of the tremendous physical, cognitive, and emotional changes that occur during this period.

## Boundaries

A major task of the first eighteen months of life is to perceive oneself as a being with boundaries, separate from other beings and objects. This occurs as the child develops the ability to pay attention to herself and what she experiences, and to mentally store the meanings she attributes to those experiences.

When the child reaches adolescence she is initially unsure where the boundary around herself is located. She is incensed by any *invasion* by another into what she considers her private space. On the other hand, she frequently invades the physical, intellectual, and emotional space of others in many ways, with impunity—in the volume of music she plays, dropping her belongings indiscriminately about the house, and the ridicule she feels free to visit on family members. In order to feel complete, she may incorporate substances into her being (food, alcohol, drugs) or she may merge her identity with a romantic partner, cult ideology, and/or membership.

Adolescents are very concerned with their bodies and appearance, asserting bodily independence through choice of hairstyle, clothing, and language. The adolescent also denies his body and its demands because his body is too real. This affects his use of showers, deodorants, and perfumes and use of rude body positions and crude outbursts. Whenever parents object to any of the above, the adolescent responds with rage, believing that the parents are trying to control his body. Adolescents somatize emotional issues (the tendency to experience and express psychological distress through physical symptoms). They are "love sick" and worry over acne, constipation, and other physical ailments.

Real two-way intimacy is a threat to the adolescent's identity and the boundary between herself and another, because she can't sustain a balance between being too close to (evoking fear of merger with another) and too far (evoking fear of abandonment and being alone). She isn't comfortable letting another *in* by sharing her thoughts and feelings with that person, nor is she comfortable living in isolation.

She believes others are as obsessed with, and as admiring and as critical, of her behavior and appearance as she is. She fails to differentiate between what she believes to be attractive in herself and what others actually admire. It takes years for adolescents to achieve cohesive and integrated perceptions of and beliefs about themselves, others, and the world.

## Paying Attention

Adolescents tend to focus excessively on one thing at a time—school, peers, job, or romantic relationships. Ability to easily shift their focus between activities and interests only gradually appears. An adolescent's ability to sustain focus on something of his choosing can be extraordinary. However sustained focus on a task of little interest to the adolescent is only intermittently available. He pays diminished attention to the world and the people around him. He is much less capable than the child or adult of appreciating that which is not immediately demanding his attention.

## Learning

She vacillates between wanting to learn everything about a single subject and disinterest in learning much at all. Males seem to prefer academic subjects involving numerical and spatial relations; females seem to prefer subjects involving human relationships and verbal skills. Whether this is inherent or due to influences during the early years of life and school is not clear.

The consequences of limitations in learning ability and/or performance, and the consequences of ineffectively addressed learning differences, may exert a major influence on the adolescent's self-esteem and his or her hope of successfully moving into the adult world.

## Changes in Cognitive Abilities

Piaget referred to the cognitive skills gained in this stage as the period of Formal Operations. Initially the adolescent can find logical solutions to concrete problems. As cognitive structures in the brain mature, the adolescent can logically solve all classes of problems. He/she can:

a. Simultaneously consider relationships among several different properties (for example, density, size, and weight).
b. See all possible variations of a problem and systematically test solutions to them.
c. Think and conceptualize abstractly, make inferences, and consider multiple aspects of an issue.
d. Use inductive and deductive reasoning, make and evaluate hypotheses.
e. Consider in silence—or argue, challenge, and debate—the implications of proposals.
f. Think about and express highly abstract views.
g. Use propositional phrases like "if so and so," then "such and such."
h. Consider problems with many factors operating simultaneously (e.g. how many different arrangements of sixteen bottle caps are possible).
i. Work with a set of symbols (algebra).
j. Understand that words can have different meanings; understand metaphors, double entendres, and cartoons.
k. Argue a point of view even though he knows the premise is untrue.

The adolescent thinks and expresses highly abstract views, uses *either/or* thinking, and is no longer rooted in the concrete world of here and now. She can treat her own thought as an object, allowing her to introspect and reflect on her own mental and personality traits. However, she lacks insight into herself, and so she fails to perceive contradictions, incongruities, and absurdities in her thinking.

Her thinking is egocentric. She doesn't distinguish between her own conceptualizations and wishes, and those of the rest of her family and society at large. Therefore, she thinks others should immediately line up with her beliefs, while she is simultaneously one hundred percent resistant to accepting the ideas of another.

Her thinking is also idealistic. She can imagine ideal families and societies, and thinks that in a brief moment, without effort, things can move from an idea to reality. She thinks adults have *sold out* and are hypocrites who are not putting their values into practice. However, she has little concept of how changes can actually be effected, and little interest in working towards this goal, especially if it might require any sacrifice on her part. For example, she may voice strong belief that money should immediately be shared equally in society, while remaining comfortable spending all of her money on clothes and downloading music.

Adolescents use their increased thinking abilities to scrutinize and continually question and judge the behavior and values of their parents. To the dismay of parents, they do so with uncomfortably close accuracy, in a routinely disparaging tone. Fourteen-year-old Ken's parent were arguing once again about some issue they both deemed important. Ken walked into the room, listened for a few moments, and then announced in a disgusted tone, "You two sound like kindergarteners fighting over a tricycle!" Adolescents often think a good deal about competition and vacillate between fascination with it, and abhorrence of it.

## Reworking of the Hallmark Skills of the Second Stage of Development

### Range of Feelings

The adolescent usually has easy access to a full range of all four feelings: happy, sad, angry, and scared. However, the predominant one most often directed at parents is some degree of anger. His more positive feelings tend to be reserved for interactions with others.

According to Leo Maddow, adolescence is almost synonymous with anger on the part of both parents and adolescent. The adolescent can find little to like about his parents and believes that they are against him or want to control him. This causes him to be angry with them. This is a less than conscious way to block awareness of the positive feelings he has for them at times. He is compelled to separate from them in order to consolidate his own identity as an individual and move out into the wider world on his own. In their frequent clashes, neither adolescent nor parent feels much satisfaction, nor that they have *won* the argument.

The adolescent adopts a rebellious *who needs you* attitude, and seeks to have only superficial contact with his parents to get distance from aspects of the parents he perceives as similar to himself.

The adolescent has an unrealistic concern about his vulnerability. He tends to feel invincible, "I will never have a car wreck, get a girl pregnant, or get an STD," in spite of all available statistical and real-life evidence to the contrary. Instead, he believes his parents are unrealistically concerned with his safety and well-being and/or lack sufficient trust in his ability to keep himself safe. He generally responds to their worry with anger and disgust. He is likely to be unaware of the probable consequences of his actions.

Like the child of eighteen to thirty-six months of age who goes almost instantly from a happy "Me do it myself!" announcement to a total meltdown because it's nap time, the adolescent undergoes rapid changes in intense feeling states in short periods of time. For example, an hour after demonstrating an adult level of empathy and efficient action in response to a flat tire while driving a younger sibling to the doctor, sixteen-year-old Tim had a screaming fit appropriate for a four-year-old, because his parents refused him permission to attend a party on the weekend. That fit was interrupted by a phone call from a friend of Tim's in emotional crisis, and Tim immediately responded like a trained grief counselor.

## Reality Testing and Realistically Assessing Personal Responsibility

Adolescents have difficulty both acknowledging responsibility for their failures to take needed actions, and feeling good about their successful efforts. They frequently misunderstand the feelings and behaviors of others.

The struggle during this period is to successfully move the parent-adolescent relationship from one that is based on the parent determining and enforcing responsibilities assigned to the adolescent, to one based on reciprocal responsiveness. In other words, to change to a "Let's each contribute to what needs to be done in the situation" relationship based on empathic cooperation.

This transition is aided if the adolescent, encouraged by parents, can successfully manage increasing responsibility for management of his or her personal life and contribute in positive ways to family life.

The adolescent often feels she is being tested and pushed by the demands and values of parents, school, and peers. She may find it difficult to take a stand and sustain her own position. Therefore she pushes her parents to see if they can hold their ground on their values and demands in the face of her ridicule.

Since the adolescent's reality testing is being reworked, it is important for parents to determine which of their rules are based on their values and which are based their own idiosyncrasies. They need to be prepared to stand their ground on behalf of both while the adolescent attacks or laughs about either or both. In addition, they need to distinguish between requests and demands and insist on performance of the latter.

The adolescent is often told not to act on the powerful sexual drive that frequently overtakes her thoughts, feelings, and body. According to psychoanalytic theory, the adolescent attacks parental values because she is unable to say what she really wishes to say: "You tell me not to have sex, but you don't tell me how I am to manage my sexual desires! Find you never showed me or told me how to behave sexually."

Peer group membership is sought and prized as a source of self-esteem and as a venue to practice being a reliable and responsible member of a group outside of the adolescent's family. It is also sought because group membership blurs awareness of personal responsibility, which is difficult for the adolescent to realistically assess, acknowledge, and carry out. Adolescents are torn between internal opposing desires to make their own decisions, follow rules set by the group, or to rebel against the group's rules.

The adolescent may be completely unwilling to follow reasonable parental requirements for maintaining personal safety, but may follow the unwise lead of peers without hesitation. The danger is that a decision to blindly follow can have catastrophic consequences, without the opportunity for a *re-do*.

On the other hand, the adolescent may be unable to decline an invitation to an activity about which she has doubts. Instead, she *messes up* at home, and her parents impose restrictions preventing her participation in the activity. The adolescent is then angry with her parents for trying to *control* her. She wants her parents to explain and justify their position on the matter so she can find fault with their decision, in order to highlight the difference between herself and her parents. She is unable to recognize her internal conflict between desire and the responsibilities that come with the privilege of making her own action decisions.

Some parents, when deciding whether or not to acquiesce to an adolescent's desire to participate in a particular activity, find it helpful to pay attention to the way that permission is sought. If asked, "Can I go to the party on Friday night?" the parents might consider playing "the heavy" and refusing permission. On the other hand, if told, "Harry and I have saved up money to take the train to the city to see the auto show," parents might consider saying yes. In the first instance, the adolescent is asking, indicating probable internal conflict with the plan, versus telling in the second instance, indicating internal comfort with the plan.

## Reworking of the Hallmark Skills of the Third Stage of Development

### Time

Increased thinking skills allow the adolescent to see a host of alternatives, and decision making becomes a problem. He wants to know why parents think this and that, and is ready to debate all the drawbacks and virtues of the all alternatives. His new indecisiveness prompts increased dependency on his parents and peers, but he internally rebels against accepting any decisions made by another.

Music is often very important to the adolescent. The predominate element in it is rhythm, a combination of some amount of strength and some frequency of time. These two elements are needed to accomplish any task. Lyrics frequently involve time, and leaving, being left, love lasting forever, betrayal, as well as descriptions of real events that significantly impact the lives of adolescents. The adolescent may use music to help get a job done, but the adolescent is far more interested in hearing or fantasizing or talking about work than he is about actually doing it.

He is reworking his sense of both physical and social timing. He has difficulty considering time as an important dimension of living and loving. He simultaneously believes that the passage of time alone will significantly change things, and that things will never change. He feels both old before his time and like a baby. He is unable to effectively use available time. He makes unrealistic assessments of how much time and effort is required to accomplish a goal—for instance, to complete school work on time or to maintain a friendship. He is often impatient and quits a project before completing it.

Like the three- and four-year-old, he wants immediate gratification without effort on his part. He wants immediate change in his parents, while not seeing any need for change on his part. He concentrates on his desire to do something now, rather than on possible or probable consequences to his action choices.

## Organizational Skills

He needs opportunities to use and develop organizational skills, such as time management, task sequencing, and empathic cooperation with others. He needs to be seen as acceptable and competent by others in the world outside his family. He needs to have his thoughts, feelings, and actions accepted and appreciated by others through participation in meaningful employment, through athletics, school and group activities, and/or community service.

Parents find it quite frustrating when their adolescent is able to circumvent a parental restriction. However, this may show creativity and good organizational skills. If at all possible, this should be accepted. For example, fourteen-year-old Keith's mother was fed up with the way her son had been talking to her. Consequently, she withdrew her offer to drive him to the neighboring college town to watch a football game the coming weekend. Instead of having a verbal fit, Keith got on his phone and found another way to get to and from the game. His mother wisely accepted this solution and managed to find a balance between irritation that Keith had escaped a just consequence for his bad behavior and relief that Keith kept his upset in check and effectively solved his problem.

## Action Decisions

In the adolescent's attempts to establish a solid sense that she is an individual who differs from her parents in important ways, she chooses romantic relationships, friends, activities, behaviors, and clothing styles that highlight the differences between herself and her parents. While acceptance from others is important, the adolescent also needs acceptance from her parents for things about her that the parents do not like, in order to feel that the person she is becoming is acceptable to them. For example, if academic performance is adequate, the adolescent's learning style and study habits should be accepted.

Dating is a source of recreation and status, and of practicing mate selection. It is a way of gaining information about herself (aspects of herself, both positive and negative, are attributed to the partner) and information about others. At times the attachment may in fact be to the partner's family.

She idealizes those on whom she has crushes. Attachment tends to begin suddenly, and is accompanied by her belief that this love will last forever, and a strong desire to spend every possible moment with that person. The relationship most often also ends quite suddenly, because no person can match the ideal created in the adolescent's fantasy, and she has spotty compassion for shortcomings in herself and her partner. She either despairs that she will ever find another partner, or quickly begins another equally intense relationship she believes will last forever.

If parents accept the friend or romantic partner chosen by the adolescent, it models parental acceptance of the person the adolescent feels herself to be at that time. However, parents should be wary of becoming over involved in the adolescent's romantic relationship since it is likely to end abruptly.

It is also important that the parents affirm the positive action decisions of the adolescent, and demonstrate active interest in, and support of, the adolescent's needs and interests. Too often parents focus almost exclusively on their offspring's unacceptable behavior. Attempts to control and subjugate the adolescent's behavior are doomed to failure and greatly exacerbate negative feelings on both sides.

If the adolescent's room is a chaotic disaster except for a salt water fish tank, comment positively on the fish tank, not the chaos. Insist that he keep his door closed instead. Letting her keep her room to her own standards (with only minimum requirements for health, safety, and cleanliness) makes her more willing to meet parental standards for shared space in the rest of the home.

A possible guide for parents concerned about their adolescent's companions and activities is for them to evaluate her action decisions compared to those of her chosen companions. Is your child the most daring? The most timid? The voice of reason? The most outlandishly or most conservatively dressed? Or is your offspring somewhere in the middle, compared to her compatriots?

Who is your child when away from the family? One parent sent her daughter, Tanya, off to her boyfriend's senior prom in an appropriate dress, only to hear from one of the chaperoning parents the next day that Tanya and her boyfriend had made quite an impression in their matching pink and black leopard spotted leotards and tights, and their black leather jackets!

The adolescent will frequently reject the ideas and values of her own parents, while loudly approving of similar values held by adults of whom her parents approve. June and her parents seemed to clash almost constantly. However, good friends of June's parents, at whose home June spent a lot of time as a babysitter, reported that June was a "dream," unlike their own teenager, with whom those parents were having difficulties.

## Family Life

Scheduling time together: It is still important to have time set aside for the parents as individuals and as a couple, for the family as a whole, and for Special Time with each adolescent. The adolescent is likely to be less than enthusiastic about Special Time with a parent, but insisting on it (for the parent, not for the adolescent) sends the important and clear message that the parent cares about, and is interested in, the adolescent as a person. Most adolescents are interested in eating, and if attention to any other family members and electronic devices are banned for a shared meal or late evening snack, that can serve as Special Time.

## Parent-Adolescent Interactions

There is a general rule of thumb that says that parents are doing well if they are getting along fifty percent of the time with their adolescent. Friction between parents and adolescents for a significant part of this stage is almost constant. Clashes between adolescents who have more autonomy and younger ones who can't tolerate sarcasm (due to lack of abstract thinking) are also frequent. Friction provides emotional heat—and distance. Here are some things that may help:

Allow the adolescent to keep his belongings the way he wishes to keep them, in whatever space is his, whether in his own room or part of a room shared with other siblings.

Distinguish clearly between a request and a demand. Make it clear that the adolescent needs to attend to family obligations first, school and other obligations next.

Negotiate a contract for any household responsibilities assigned to the adolescent. This should include a detailed description of what is involved in the completed assignment, and a deadline for work completion. Parental reminders or comments should not be made until the deadline for job completion is reached.

Before imposing consequences for incomplete work, comment on whatever part of the assignment was adequately completed. Avoid using the word "you." Inquire why the remainder was not completed, making the assumption that the adolescent's intentions were the best rather than the worst. Describe the area in which the difficulty occurred in terms of developmental skills needed to complete any job. For example:

   a. Too much or not enough energy was mobilized to complete the job effectively and efficiently.

b. Sufficient attention was not paid to all relevant job elements.

c. Specified responsibilities were not performed and/or notice was not given that the job couldn't be completed satisfactorily prior to the deadline for completion, so no alternate plan was made and agreed upon.

d. Time and resources were inadequately managed to allow job completion within specified time limits.

Any consequence leveled on the adolescent should be announced when the parent has taken time to calmly consider what it should be. The consequence should not fall on the parents or other family members, nor impact any membership obligations the adolescent has to other groups, such as athletic teams or employers. A well-chosen consequence leveled on an adolescent allows the parent to put the responsibility for its occurrence on the adolescent's own choice of behavior. To this the parent can express the hope that the adolescent will make a different choice in the future.

After assigning a job or imposing a consequence it is helpful if the parents disregard whatever comes forth from the adolescent's mouth, and instead pay attention to whether the adolescent is moving in the appropriate direction and beginning to work on the task.

Unlike an angry young child, the adolescent has a number of ways to argue forcefully against, or to circumvent, parental behavioral constraints. "You can't make me!" and "I don't care!" are frequently heard refrains. When setting a limit displeasing to the adolescent, the parent can remind the adolescent that he will have the chance to do far differently than his parent when he is the parent of an adolescent of his own, but that right now it is the parent's turn to do the best the parent can.

When the adolescent requests permission to participate in an activity, the parent is on sound footing to say that the request will be considered only if the adolescent will accept parental refusal—should that be the outcome—without having an angry fit. Otherwise, the parent will refuse permission immediately without even hearing the request.

Use of raw power ("I'm the parent and you'll do what I say!") becomes increasingly ineffectual during this stage. Parental power is diminishing as the adolescent's intellectual, physical, and emotional power is increasing. The adolescent will frequently mention this new reality, to the extreme discomfort of the parents. Limit setting by the parents needs to transition into mutual consideration and cooperation—from parents being in control to negotiated, increasing autonomy for both parents and adolescent.

If parents disagree on how appropriate a consequence or a course of action is for their adolescent, they need to discuss it out of the adolescent's awareness, and agree which parent will handle the matter and which parent will remain out of the situation. Be prepared for the adolescent to ridicule parental conferencing; he may attempt to exploit it as a weakness, perceiving that neither parent is strong enough to take a stand on his or her own.

Life tasks such as effectively managing academic study time and meeting basic food, sleep, and clothing needs increasingly fall on the adolescent's shoulders, whether the parents like this or not. It is wise to set mid-level requirements in these areas, leaving room for the adolescent to gain self-esteem from exceeding them.

If parents have evidence that academics, social activities, and household and outside work are all being managed responsibly enough, it is best to let the adolescent pursue them in his own way, giving the adolescent more and more freedom from parental restrictions. Parents need to be clear about their own stance concerning use of alcohol and drugs and sexual behavior, but should expect that a certain amount of experimentation by their children is likely. Again, the emphasis should be on the adolescent behaving responsibly.

At times, the adolescent will likely find himself in situations he knows he should leave. It can be most helpful if he is encouraged to call his parents in this case, to receive help leaving the situation without questioning or recrimination from the parents. Some parents have found it helpful to tell the adolescent that he should always feel free to say that his immediate presence is required at home. Adolescent and parent may agree upon a pre-arranged signals (for example, the adolescent sends a text message or by calling the parent's phone twice and hanging up after one ring). This signal indicates the adolescent's desire that the parent call him and demand that he immediately return home.

Parents need to look for opportunities to comment positively on the adolescent's ideas, demonstrated skills, and chosen pursuits. This is very difficult to do when a good deal of his behavior is annoying to the parents. In addition, if the adolescent agrees with a parent, he isn't sure he is a different person than that parent.

For example, a parent might comment that the adolescent's outfit or hairstyle looks great, or that the adolescent is really becoming very attractive. Such a comment is likely to evoke an immediate refutation by the adolescent. Instead of getting into a pointless, winless argument, the parent should simply acknowledge that he/she and the adolescent have very different perceptions about the matter. The same refutation by the adolescent will follow the parent's commenting that the adolescent's hair style, clothing, etc., looks awful. In this case the adolescent's refutation is likely to include the charge that unlike all other parents, his parent is clueless about the latest style!

## The Ending of Adolescence

There is no clear ending of adolescence in this country. Economic and educational factors are among the main factors contributing to the prolongation of this stage of development.

## Self-Perception – If Things Go Well Enough

In the face of the upcoming loss of the parent-child relationship that both parties have gotten used to over the years, parent and adolescent kick sand in each other's faces in order to produce, accentuate, and perpetuate the familiar, highly intense feelings they have had for and about one another. Friction simultaneously causes closeness/warmth and distance/separation. Often it feels easier to leave someone if you think you don't need, or even like them. Few families confront directly the sadness inherent in this major change in family structure and dynamics.

If all goes well enough, the relationship shifts from one of parental control to one of negotiated, increasing autonomy in action (versus reaction) for both adolescent and parent. The adolescent prepares to leave home, the parents prepare for life without their offspring.

The adolescent's personality and sense of identity has been consolidated. She has a set of moral values that guides her action choices. There is a diminishing disparity between her internal world of ideals and the goals she sets for life *out in* the world.

The adolescent has had opportunities to connect information she's learned with information and ideas she will need in her adult life. For example, she can consider implications of proposals in silence, argue, debate, and challenge any proposition. She has had adequate opportunities to try out abilities and develop skills she will need as an adult to successfully fit into the larger society.

She has a realistic appreciation of the possibility of success and failure in her future endeavors. She takes responsibility for the management of her own intellectual, emotional, and practical living on both a daily and long-term basis.

She possesses the skills to enable her to find satisfactory adult relationships with others because she is tolerant of differences in opinions, and accepts her own limitations and those of others. She sees others as they are, rather than as idealized or demonized versions of themselves.

The relationship she has with her parents is based on mutual empathy. Her parents and she seek each other out for activities of mutual and individual choosing, and converse as individuals, rather than as parent and child. When she returns for a visit to her parents' home she is treated as an honored guest. She is accepted as having adult status and parents and now adult child are considerate of the differences in how they each choose to conduct their lives.

## Difficulties Originating in This or Earlier Stages That May Appear in Adolescence or Later

Difficulties stemming from the parents' own adolescent experiences: As discussed earlier in this writing, unfinished adolescent issues in a parent, long out of his/her conscious awareness, may emerge—and this can add significantly to family difficulties. For example, if one of the adolescent's parents experienced significant disapproval or rejection from his/her own parents, this parent may be too needy for acceptance from the adolescent child to set appropriate limits, or to let the adolescent child appropriately venture forth into the larger world on his own.

Difficulties can be mitigated by examination of what the conflicted parent liked and didn't like about his or her own adolescent experiences. Sharing some of that information with the adolescent child increases adult-appropriate *person-to-person* rather than *parent-to-adolescent* communication between them. If possible, the conflicted parent should talk with his/her own parents (the adolescent's grandparents) about the conflicted parent's unfinished adolescent issues.

The idea is not to condemn, condone, or argue about what the conflicted parent—or the grandparents—thought or did. Rather, it is to listen and to try to understand how each person thought that what they did was the best they could do at the time. Ideally, the things that were beneficial should be acknowledged. More difficult, and more important, is having the grandparents be willing to acknowledge that some of what occurred made the conflicted parent of the adolescent sad and angry.

Unacknowledged or denied entirely, the parents' left over feelings of upset may be unintentionally and unhelpfully visited on their adolescent.

It is unhelpful if the parents have separated and both parents and adolescent are dating. The adolescent wants the generational boundary in place so that he can push against it. It is also unhelpful if one parent is so upset about the separation that consciously or unconsciously the adolescent is pressured to supply inordinate emotional energy and time supporting the very upset parent. In acrimonious divorce proceedings, parents may have little time and/or emotional energy to provide adequate support for the concerns and interests of the adolescent.

If the parents are separated or divorced, the time the adolescent spends with each parent is limited, and conflict over the amount of time they will spend together is a given. The adolescent wants his parent to be at home as an anchor while he focuses on social activities with his peers. The potential areas of difficulty are likely to increase if remarriage occurs during this time.

The parents are living with the consequences of their life choices. They have to manage feelings about their own diminishing sexual attractiveness, attraction towards their own adolescent, and satisfaction with their own adult work and affection life. If the parents are relatively satisfied with their own lives, the adolescent is encouraged to believe he has the real possibility of creating a satisfactory life for himself.

The birth order of the adolescent—whether the child is first or last in the family—can have a significant influence. So can whether he or she is the "special one" to one or both of the parents, or if he/she has a particular designated role to play in the family (e.g. the one who will fail, the one who will not leave home, or is the one who will "make up" for financial or emotional difficulties of the parents).

Parental behavior is under close and judgmental scrutiny by the adolescent. Consequently, irresponsible behavior on the part of the parents can negatively impact action decisions the adolescent makes.

If a parent dies during this period, the adolescent may not be able to give up his idealized view of that parent. He may feel that he has caused or contributed to the parent's death. His hope for his own future may be damaged, or he may look for the lost parent in a mate upon whom he can visit his anger at his parent for dying and therefore deserting him. Pat's father had died when Pat was seventeen. Some years later it dawned on Pat that over the intervening years, he had acquired four close friends each of whom strongly resembled his father in some significant way. His relationship with each of them strongly resembled the relationship he had experienced with his father.

Significant or inadequately addressed learning difficulties, inadequate educational opportunities, discrimination, inadequate academic effort on the adolescent's part, or lack of economic opportunities can all negatively impact his ability to attain goals set by himself, parents, or society. They can all hamper his ability to fit into an adult role or to view of himself as an acceptable and independent enough person to achieve and maintain a loving adult relationship. For example, inability to adequately acquire abstract thinking may leave the adolescent incapable of literally—or figuratively—leaving home.

Presence of a chronic or acute medical condition can lead to depression about needing help with his functioning, and difficulty seeing himself living independently.

He may seek allegiance to a cult as a way to avoid struggling for an internal balance between ambivalence in his thoughts and feelings, which is essential for an independent adult life. Allegiance to the cult leader who knows "the truth and the way to live" involves relinquishing personal responsibility for his thinking, feeling, and action decisions, in exchange for finding his place in the world. It can result from either parental rules that are too numerous and/or strict, or a significant lack of such rules.

Substance abuse or addiction to work, gambling, or other activity may be used to obtain temporary relief from pain or stress arising from either internal or external sources. This is reminiscent of the experience of an infant, whose unhappiness can be temporarily totally relieved by the presence of his mother.

Pregnancy can be a way for the adolescent girl to attempt to resolve the conflict between a strong desire for independence and not being ready to assume the responsibility for such independence. She may believe that true independence lies in having a baby who will depend on her and love her because of that dependency on her.

Somatic symptoms may develop if there isn't adequate permission for the adolescent to express the upset she or he is experiencing: for example, if a parent's usual refrain is, "You're too sensitive," "Don't dwell on the negative," or "Don't be a baby; everyone has problems."

Obtaining professional help should be considered if any of the following persist for a significant period of time:

   a. He or she is not connected or passionately interested in anything, and lacks hope for the future.

   b. He or she doesn't feel important to anyone.

   c. There is no adult particularly concerned with the adolescent.

d. His or her interpersonal relations involve extremes in unacceptable behaviors, or activities that indicate extreme views.
e. Relationships with significant others are based on power not empathy.
f. He or she lacks realistic intellectual perspective on ideas, people, and events.
g. There are significant, ongoing problems with family members, peers, school, and/or work.

# In Closing

I offer some parting words of encouragement. Yes, human development and personality formation is a complex process and parenting involves hard work. But there are rewards that can be long lasting, as well as enjoyable surprises as each child grows and develops his or her unique personality. Parents often experience richer, more deeply textured lives as a result of raising their children and gain a more compassionate, accepting, less judgmental perspective on the behavior of themselves and others.

To my way of thinking, a good-enough parent is one who tries to make the best choices he or she can as each day unfolds in its often unpredictable way. Time is found to spend regularly occurring, enjoyable time with each child. The inevitability of both good and bad days is accepted, and the good-enough parent is kind to him or herself when the latter occurs.

Having a good sense of humor, and one or two adults with whom one can honestly and openly talk, is of invaluable assistance in coping with difficult moments and situations. I will leave you with one last story.

My neighbor Lolly and I were chatting across our common back yard fence one summer, Saturday afternoon. Our respective husbands wouldn't be home until evening and each of us had been having a rough day with our children. A misplaced sandal had delayed a food shopping trip and intermittent squabbles had broken out repeatedly in both households. Edith the hamster had turned the day topsy turvy during a brief escape from her cage. It was only four p.m., and bedtime for Lolly's three children (two, four, and seven) and mine (two and four), seemed a very long way off.

Lolly and I were fraying at the ends of our respective ropes. We decided that rather than continue the downward spiral of the day, isolated with our respective children, both generations would be better off if we joined forces in my back yard where the kids could splash in the kiddie pool, play on the swings, and eat sandwiches for dinner. Lolly and I could sit in the shade and hopefully cobble together a lighter and more positive spin on the situation than either was experiencing alone.

The plan worked well and soon we were all having a good time. I had made a chocolate cake for dessert and we asked Lolly's seven-year-old son, Calef, to get the cake from my kitchen and bring it into the back yard. Lolly and I were sitting with our backs to the kitchen door. We heard Calef exclaim quietly, "Oh no!" as he stumbled down the three steps leading from the kitchen to the yard. We all turned and stared. Miraculously, he regained firm footing on the ground. But his chest was now thickly coated with globs of chocolate cake and icing.

Lolly and I locked gazes in the silence that held us all for a few seconds. That gaze said, "Thank goodness we are together in this." Alone, each of would probably have reacted to the situation with some form of exploding exasperation. Instead, we just started laughing as the children adapted appropriately to the situation by swiping bits of cake and icing off Calef's chest (quite clean from swimming) with their hands and fingers, stuffing them into their happy, waiting mouths.

# Acknowledgments

Information in this book was gathered over many years of being a spouse, parent, nursery school teacher and director, creative arts psychotherapist, school counselor, marriage and family therapist, and teacher and supervisor of psychotherapists. This book would not have been possible without the invaluable information and insights shared with me by the adults and children with whom it was my privilege and pleasure to live, know, teach, and work. I am passing the information along in the hope that it may help those adults currently engaged in the caring, protection, and guidance of growing children, helping them effectively deal with difficulties between family members before they reach a crisis point.

    I am indebted to my husband's forbearance during months of my attachment to my computer and to a myriad of notes. And to Sara Lynn Valentine for her ability to round the corners of rough sentences. Ideas in this book would never have landed on printed pages without her skill and invaluable assistance.

# About the Author

Sherry Walker lives in Durango, Colorado where she writes children's books, makes pottery, and roams the countryside with her husband, Herb. Her children, biological and informally adopted, range in age from forty to fifty-five, and her grandchildren, from one to twenty. At seventy-five, she still greets every morning with curiosity about what the day will bring.

Sherry's long list of credentials include thirty-five years in private practice as a psychotherapist; Clinical Instructor and Supervisor in the Creative Arts In Therapy Department at Hahnemann University; Adjunct Professor in the graduate division of Chestnut Hill College; Senior Staff Therapist and Clinical Instructor at The Marriage Council of Philadelphia, also known as the Division of Family Study of the Medical School of the University of Pennsylvania; Instructor in the Department of Psychology at Fort Lewis College, and Child Development Specialist at The Child Development Center at Fort Lewis College; and a Clinical and Approved Supervisor Member of the American Association of Marriage and Family Therapists (AAMFT).

www.ingramcontent.com/pod-product-compliance
Lightning Source LLC
Chambersburg PA
CBHW071625080526
**44588CB00010B/1267**